WILD WOMEN ON THE WATER

KEYS FOR SURVIVAL

(A Handbook for Enjoying the Island Lifestyle)

- More Than a Cookbook, More Than a Survival Manual
- Tips & Hints, Some Life-Saving
- True Stories & Adventures, Humor, History, & Trivia

By Gail Underwood Feddern

PAGE PUBLISHING, INC.
New York, NY

First originally published by Page Publishing, Inc. 2018

*Copyedited by Henry A. Feddern, Tanya T. Feddern-Bekcan,
Gloria Vinskey, and Cristine Pistol.*

*The author, publisher, editors, websites, and people contributing to this
book shall not be held liable for any damage to property or harm or
death of any persons who followed the information in this book. The
sincere intent of this book is to help people survive dangerous situations;
however, there are no guarantees in life. Sometimes someone can do
everything right and still end up dead. Conversely, another person facing
certain death can emerge from that situation virtually unscathed.*

ISBN 978-1-64082-419-5 (Paperback)
ISBN 978-1-64082-420-1 (Digital)

Printed in the United States of America

ACKNOWLEDGMENTS

Cover: The *Nautilimo*, stuffed with several Wild Women on the Water, cruising and posing on Florida Bay. I want to thank Captain Joe Fox for letting us use his unique watercraft. (It probably helps that he's married to Wild Woman on the Water Eileen Lomas-Fox!) His *Nautilimo*, skippered by Capt. Joe Fox himself, is available for charters. It makes prom dates, birthdays, and sunset cruises unforgettable experiences. You can contact him through the Islamorada Chamber of Commerce. Thank you, Peggy Moon and Mr. Stud, Debi Dorn, Pat Rosendale, Sally Stribling, Sandra Beese Whitfield, and Sylvia Miles for letting me shanghai you all to be my crew for this photo shoot. It was easy. All I had to do was ply you all with grog.

Title suggestion by Suzy Burrows. **Photo credits:** A special thank you goes out to my very talented husband, Henry A. Feddern, for taking the cover photograph, as well as some others throughout the book. Many thanks to all the Wild Women on the Water who have contributed snapshots throughout the years for our group scrapbooks; with the club's permission, I borrowed freely from them. I don't know who the photographers are, so I am unable to cite individual credits, but you will probably recognize your pictures.

Recipe credits: My deepest gratitude to those Wild Women on the Water who contributed their recipes for this project. Without your contributions, this book would not have been possible. Now you're famous, so aren't you glad you did? My apologies if I left your name off your recipe, but I gave my best effort to identify the cooks who turned in recipes without their names.

Lastly, thanks to Richard Callahan, my writing instructor at Florida Keys Community College, for teaching me how to write.

In memory of Linda McGee

01/22/1942 – 10/30/2007

CONTENTS

Founder Ruth Rich (L.) receives an Appreciation Award from Loretta Lawrence (R.) on behalf of Wild Women on the Water.

Wild Women on the Water (WWOW) was started on August 12, 1996, in Islamorada by Ruth Rich and her friends. Ruth was newly divorced. She had a boat, but she didn't know how to use it. She and her friends had the same goals: to become skilled at boatmanship and water sports, to band together out of camaraderie, to participate in social activities related to the water—and to have *fun*!

There has been a lot of water under the bridges (and over the bridges, when you consider hurricanes) since then, but the club is still going strong. In fact, it grew so much that at one point Wild

Women on the Water voted to limit its membership to 125 members! (Membership limits have since been lifted.) Some of the founding members still actively participate.

The club is also a learning experience. It has arranged for its members to learn about basic mechanics for boat owners, GPS navigation, CPR, how to throw a cast net, tie fishing tackle, and other workshops. Among the field trips, the Coast Guard station in Islamorada hosted WWOW to a picnic and taught us how to select and shoot off signal flares safely.

The club meets once a month in the Upper Keys. At most meetings, a speaker lectures on a water-oriented topic. Following the lecture or demonstration, members schedule water activities and events for the upcoming months at the regular business meeting. Any woman over eighteen is welcome to attend.

WWOW members drag their husbands and boyfriends to two annual events. One is the big Christmas party, where everyone gets to dress up. That practically never happens in the Keys, so it's a rare pleasure to see each other wearing dressy dresses instead of the shorts and bathing suits we see all year long. And don't our men look hunky in honest-to-God suits and ties! The other event is the picnic. Other than those two times, no males are allowed at WWOW events and activities.

Currently, our website is: www.wildwomenon-thewater.weebly.com.

Like us on Facebook.

Author Gail Feddern climbing the rigging of an Indonesian sailing ship on Tall Ships Day at the Port of Miami. It was a WWOW outing.

Author Gail Feddern and her marine biologist husband Dr. Henry A. Feddern about to dance the night away at a WWOW Christmas holiday party

Recipe for WWOW Overboards
(Formerly called Man Overboards)
By Cathy Carey

1/2 C. each:
pineapple rum
banana rum
coconut rum
orange rum
Bacardi dark rum
1 large can of pineapple juice
splash of blue Curacao or Midori liqueur (just
    enough to make it green)

No WWOW outing would be the same without Cathy Carey's notorious rum punch!

Helpful Tip: How to make a *Keys Coolie Cup*— nest your drink inside another cup with a cocktail napkin between the two to act as insulation.

Tourist Tips: Fish off the bridges (designated) and have fun. Know and observe the laws, and don't waste fish. Put unwanted fish back in the water, even if they're dead, for sharks and crabs to eat.

Lock your valuables in the trunk of your car unobserved, as you would before you leave your motel. Along the highway, on a side road or street, at the beach, or at a tourist attraction are all prime spots for thieves to target cars. Don't tempt them by leaving a camera, cell phone, iPod, clothes (which may contain a wallet), or anything else of value inside your car in plain sight.

Tear out and use dollar-saving coupons inside tourist publications, which you will find at restaurants, hotels, and chambers of commerce.

Don't speed *even a little bit* through Layton or Big Pine Key.

Beware of unscrupulous shops. There is a T-shirt store in Key West that asks for your credit card before he makes up your shirt. Do not give it to him. Ask him what it's going to cost. If you still want it at that price, tell him you'll pay for it when it's finished and he gives it to you. You can always claim you pay cash and don't use credit cards. Friends of mine thought they were getting a shirt like the dummy on display outside his store for $15, replete with sparkly decals. The catch is that the bare shirt is $15; *each decal* costs extra! The man threatened to call the police unless they paid the *$60 bill!* They should have let him, and then told the police he stole their credit card. Failing that, you can always dispute the charge on your credit card.

Also, when using your credit card for rentals that require a deposit, make sure you get back all the copies of the charge slip for the deposit when you return the item.

If you think you might need to return an item you bought, buy it with a credit card. Merchants are more apt to cooperate because they have to pay a percentage of the sale to the credit card company, whereas they get to keep it all when the sale is paid with cash or check. *You* have to pay a fee to stop payment on a check.

By law, the merchant has to post within plain view near his cash register a sign stating "No refunds or exchanges" if that's the case.

Don't let the clerk sneak a picture of your credit card with the camera in his cell phone; as soon as he lays the card on the counter, put your hand on top and slide it into your purse or wallet. When he hands your card back to you (usually wrapped in a receipt), immediately check to be sure it has your name on it. You don't want him to switch it with someone else's expired card.

Some of the best seafood you will ever eat is served in the Florida Keys. It is fresh, caught locally, and prepared by chefs who know how to cook fish right. I hated fish until I moved to South Florida and, for the first time, experienced *fresh* fish that was *not overcooked* and dry. My favorites are yellowtail, hog snapper / hogfish (really a wrasse), and mahi-mahi/dolphin. I also enjoy wahoo and cobia. But Keys restaurant menus list many other good local fish. If you don't see it, just ask. Other Keys delicacies you shouldn't miss are stone crab claws and Key lime pie.

Nice people work at the Kmart stores in the Keys. They won't give you a hassle, and the prices are cheaper. But if you can benefit from wise local advice, I recommend you patronize specialty stores. Dive shops will *fit* your dive gear. Your vacation costs money, so you want to have the best time you can. Do you want it ruined by a face mask that leaks because it doesn't fit your particular type of face or by fins that rub your feet raw because they're the wrong size or design for your feet? As for fishing, bait-and-tackle shops will sell you what you need, tell you where to go, and how to catch it. In my opinion, local stores are worth the little extra money they charge.

Camping on Nest Key, 2016.

**From the ramparts we watch—a view from
Fort Jefferson, at the Dry Tortugas.**

Sometimes WWOW likes to take one of the hydrofoils out of Key West for a day trip to the old Civil War fort. It's splendid snorkeling along marine encrusted outer walls of the moat, as well as on coral heads nearby. The boat crew sets up a nice picnic lunch. **Be sure, however, to bring plenty of your own water because there is none to be bought on the island.** Be prepared for a long, sometimes windy boat ride.

A Historical Note: Dr. Samuel Mudd was banished here for setting the broken leg of John Wilkes Booth, the assassin who shot and killed President Abraham Lincoln. (Supposedly, that is the origin of the expression "Your name is mud!" meaning persona non grata.)

Beware the latest spyware! The little "hole" on top is really a motion-activated wireless camera. If you see this in a public bathroom, don't touch it—just call the police.

PRIVACY

Let's talk about urban survival—'cause it can be a jungle out there! In this age of video voyeurism, people are increasingly finding their privacy violated. Weirdoes love to target women and children because they are vulnerable victims whose images can be readily sold over the Internet. You are not even safe on the street in broad daylight, surrounded by people! Some guys have tiny mirrors on their shoes or telescoping mirrors to look up women's skirts. Or they put their cell phone on the floor and pretend to tie their shoe, all the while recording up skirt. On the mainland, there are security cameras in the dressing rooms of some upscale department stores, peeping tom landlords, and motels with two-way mirrors. I really didn't think this was much of a problem in the Keys, because Keys people, although a friendly and sociable lot, value their own personal privacy so much that I believed they also respect the privacy of others. But now creeps are creeping into the Keys with their disgusting gadgets. Also, occasionally Keys people have to "get off the Rock," or else they "go Rock happy!" That means a trip to the mainland for a little R and R (rest and recreation).

So how does a girl protect herself? Wear slacks or jeans in public, or be particularly vigilant when you are wearing skirts and dresses. When inside a building, look around. Does anything look odd or out of place? Carefully examine the walls, ceilings, and pictures for holes and places that might hide the eye of a pervert or a surveillance camera or camcorder. Is there a micro cam hidden inside that smoke detector? Unfasten the cover and find out. Plug those holes with a wad of tissue. Cover the camera lens with a wad of gum or a garment you were going to try on. How do you know that's not a two-way mirror with some creep standing behind it, watching your every move as you undress or use the toilet? If you shine a flashlight at a genuine mirror, 100 percent of the light will reflect back at you; none of it will shine through, so you can't see the other side. But here is a surefire way to tell the difference between a genuine, legitimate mirror and a two-way mirror: Touch the surface of the mirror with your long fingernails or a pen or pencil. **If it's a real mirror, you will see a space between the object and the reflection. A two-way mirror will show no such space.** *Remember, if there is no space,* *leave that place!* If it's your apartment that you are concerned about, visit a spy store and talk to the sales clerk. You have a right to your privacy.

Recipe for Gloria's Surprise Cake
By Gloria Crum

Preheat oven to 350 degrees.
Mix:
1 box golden yellow cake mix
1 pkg. instant French vanilla pudding
1 C. sour cream
1 C. cooking oil
4 eggs
3/4 C. flaked coconut
3/4 C. chopped pecans
6 oz. chocolate chips (Add the chips after mixing other ingredients so they do not break up.)

Grease and flour a Bundt pan, and pour in the batter.

Bake for 55 minutes to 1 hour. Test for doneness. Cover it with icing if you like.

The girls clamored for Gloria Crum to give up her cake recipe. Simply orgasmic!

A Tackle Tip: If you don't need a large tackle box because you are just going fishing for the day, put what you need in a small rectangular plastic box. You can buy one for $1 or $2 at Kmart. Or you can recycle a container that baby wipes or personal wipes come in. It's hinged and just the right size for medium-size hard-bodied lures.

Taco Salad
(Makes two large bowls)
By Donna Hanson

3 lb. ground beef
2 pkgs. of taco seasoning mix
1 can of red kidney beans
1 head of lettuce
3 large tomatoes
1/4 C. celery, sliced thin
2 carrots, shredded
1 can of black olives, sliced
1 red or yellow bell pepper
1 small red onion
8–12 oz. of shredded cheddar cheese
one 12 oz. bag of taco-flavored Doritos
one 16 oz. bottle of Green Goddess dressing

In a pan, brown (and cook) the ground beef. Add the taco seasoning mix and kidney beans. Set aside.

Put the following ingredients in a very large bowl: Cut up the head of lettuce (remove and discard the big veins). Add the carrots, celery and sliced black olives. Cut up tomatoes and a small red or yellow bell pepper. Cut or shred the onion. On top of the mixture, add the shredded cheddar cheese. Crush the Doritos and put on top of the cheese. Pour the bottle of Green Goddess dressing on top and add the meat mixture. Mix with two large spoons.

Serve hot or cold. Tastes great even two days later, if it lasts that long. Be careful, it calls to you in the middle of the night—Donna Hanson's husband tells her so!

Twenty-Four-Degree Salad
By Judi Bray

1 head of lettuce, chopped
chopped celery—to taste
chopped scallions, at least 1 bunch
1 small bag of frozen peas
1 pkg. of shredded cheese
1 C. of mayonnaise
1/2 C. of lime juice
Bacon bits or pieces of cooked bacon, crumbled

Layer the first five ingredients in a rectangular pan. Cover with the mayo and lime juice. Top with crumpled bacon bits. Place in refrigerator overnight. Serve and enjoy.

Bow WWOW Pow-Wow

A group of Wild Women on the Water attending a Becoming an Outdoor Woman camp at Ocala, Florida. The Florida Fish and Wildlife Conservation Commission (FWC) holds workshops in the spring, fall, and winter in Ocala, Tallahassee, and West Palm Beach.

Ladies, these weekend workshops are the most outdoor fun you will ever have for the buck! For less than the cost of one night at a Miami Beach hotel, you will spend Friday, Saturday, and Sunday in an air-conditioned cabin, learn outdoor skills in the great outdoors, eat tasty chow, and enjoy extra-curricular activities in the evening (if you're not too worn out!). You will be busy every minute, and loving every second! Not to mention all the new friends you'll meet.

Sample sessions are bass fishing, fly-fishing, canoeing/kayaking, small game hunting, shooting sports, archery, wilderness survival (basic and advanced), reading the woods, the primitive chef (campfire cooking), personal safety, map and compass, boating basics, camping/backpacking, whitetail deer, handgun shooting, outdoor photography, bird-watching, bow hunting, talkin' turkey, hunter safety, black powder firearms, and wilderness first aid. Many other states besides Florida participate in the Becoming an Outdoors Woman program, but their sessions differ somewhat.

Hurricane Hash

(A hurricane meal)
By Gail Feddern

1 can of corned beef

1/2 bottle of Heinz catsup

2 rounded Tbs., more or less, of dried minced onion flakes

1 C., more or less, of dry Hungry Man instant mashed potatoes (Do not reconstitute.)

1 can of peas, drained (optional)

Pam cooking spray

Soak the onion flakes in a saucer with enough water to cover.

Spray a large pan with Pam. Open the can of corned beef, dump it into the pan, and separate it with a fork. Sprinkle in the rehydrated onion flakes. Add the instant mashed potatoes in an amount to approximately equal the volume of corned beef. Stir the mixture. Add the catsup (and peas for a one-dish meal) and mix some more. Heat over medium heat until the hash is slightly crusty on the bottom.

Usually after a hurricane, the electricity is out. The beauty of this dish is that you can prepare it from ingredients straight from the pantry rather than the refrigerator. You can cook it over a camp-fire or a gas range if you're lucky enough to own a gas stove instead of an electric stove. Of course, without refrigeration, your family has to eat it all, which they won't mind a bit, if they like hash.

EMERGENCY SOLAR SALTWATER STILLS

Let's hope not, but someday you may find your-self at sea with no potable water. What to do? Well, you can make water to drink by utilizing the principles of evaporation and condensation. Heat from the sun or a hot engine will distill impure water by evaporating it. Pure water can then be captured when it condenses against a surface.

If you are on a boat that is equipped for a marine life fisherman (the politically correct term for a tropical fish collector), you can probably improvise a solar still based on the earth ones you've seen in outdoor survival books.

You remember those, don't you? First, you dig out a hole in the ground. If you have them, put mashed succulent plants like cactus pads on the bottom—if not, you'll just have to depend on the moisture in the soil. Place a cup or bowl in the center of the hole. Then cover the hole with a sheet of vinyl (like Visqueen), Mylar (like a space blanket or a dismantled helium party balloon), Saran wrap, or maybe even raingear. Plastic or rubber, or whatever you use—*it must be flexible and vapor-proof!* (So your expensive Gore-Tex is probably *not* going to work.) Seal the perimeter with dirt. Lastly, weight down the center with a rock so that your water-proof fabric forms an inverted cone centered over the receptacle. Reseal the edges if necessary. If all is well, it will act as a funnel, and condensation will collect on the underside of the cover and drip down into your container. Voila! You have distilled water. This process of evaporation and condensation takes a while because it depends upon a change in temperature, so you might have to wait until dew forms at night to hasten the operation.

On a boat at sea, you can simulate the hole-in-the-ground solar still. Instead of an earthen hole, substitute a bucket. White five-gallon buckets are commonly found on boats. For your vinyl sheet, use a tropical fish bag, either half bag or full bag. Your cup or bowl should be heavy so it doesn't float; ceramic is ideal. First, dip the bucket into the sea, retaining only an inch or two of seawater, because the water level must be below the edge of your collection container. *Do not use your cup or bowl to dip seawater unless you wipe it clean again, because you don't want to contaminate your distilled catch water with salt.* Instead of seawater, you could use seaweed, preferably crushed. Put the bucket in a sunny spot. Next, carefully place the cup or bowl in the center of the bucket. Arrange the plastic fish bag so that the bottom of it is inside the bucket above the catch container. Using tape, seal the edges of the bag tightly against the outside wall of the bucket. You might have to trim the bag or remove the wire handle to get a proper seal. You can use a 1- or 2-lb. diving weight or a handful of sinkers to center the apex of the bag over your cup or bowl.

This method produces fresh water but not very much, and it takes a long time. I found a better, much simpler idea is to just use Ziploc bags and saucers, items commonly found in your average cabin cruiser. *Only this time, put the seawater in the saucers, inside the bags, set them out in the sun, and zip them shut.* In a short while, freshwater will begin to sweat on the inside of the bags. Carefully unzip each one, remove the saucer without spilling, and either *drink directly from each* bag, or zip it shut to hold for later.

Roasted Potato Salad
By Eileen Lomas Fox

6–7 red potatoes, cut into cubes and roasted
1 small red onion, diced
4 sticks of celery, diced
1/2 lb. of bacon
1 or 2 hard-boiled eggs, chopped
1/4 C. vinegar
1/4 C. sugar
salt to taste
black pepper to taste
paprika to taste
dry mustard

In a pan, fry the bacon until it's crisp. Remove the bacon and chop it up. Put equal amounts of vinegar and sugar and 1/4 tsp. dry mustard in the pan and bring to a boil. Pour over the potato mixture. Mix in the bacon pieces, onion, celery, and hard-boiled eggs. Sprinkle with salt, pepper, and paprika.

SHARK MAMMOGRAM
(A true adventure)
By Gail Feddern

The weather was far from calm, but my husband Henry and I went snorkeling in three or four feet of water, inshore on the bay side, just south of Tavernier Creek, in view of a row of houses a quarter of a mile away. It was there that a shark attacked me.

Don't worry—it was a twelve-inch baby nurse shark. OK, OK, I admit I was trying to catch it in my collecting bag to show Henry. I never touched it, but it had enough of my fooling around, it glared at me with its pale green eyes and *charged* me! Now, nurse sharks are relatively harmless, having mostly tiny teeth and molars; they like to suck things like shellfish. It glommed onto my right breast.

I grabbed it behind the head and held on because I didn't want it to get away until I showed Henry. It was a cute little guy, brown with its baby spots, so it must have been a newborn. I held on tight. The shark held on tight. After a while, I realized I needn't bother, because it had me more than I had it. Its bite was like a pinch (no worse than a mammogram), and wasn't hurting a whole lot. Then I tried to pull it off. Uh-uh. It *wasn't* letting go!

So I swam over to Henry, this Alien-like appendage flopping around on my chest. After my dear husband quit laughing at me, he tried to pull it off. *Ouch!* Nothing doing.

So we swam back to the boat. Henry got into the boat while I stayed in the water. I proposed to take off my dive skins and leave it on the gulf bottom, figuring the shark would grow bored, release, and swim off. Henry thought that wasn't a good plan because of all the gear I'd have to remove, but he didn't have a better one. So off with the fins. Off with the booties. Off with the dive skins. Uh-oh. That damned little shark had hold of my bathing suit, too, and wasn't letting go! I had no choice. I looked around to see if there were any other boaters nearby.

Off with my bathing suit! Yikes! There I am, Gail the Whale, in the altogether, an immense amount of white skin with a red one-inch hickey on my right boob. I must have looked like Moby Dick with a birthmark! My sympathetic husband is rolling around laughing so hard, he nearly capsizes the boat!

I try to hide behind the stern of the boat, but Henry is tormenting me. He's taken a blunt-tip knife, and he's pried that bulldog shark off my dive clothes, and now he's got that nasty little nurse shark in his hands, and he's jabbing at me with it and threatening to let it nurse my other booby! I'm screaming, laughing, and hollering at him, and I don't know what to do. I can't stay behind the boat stern forever. There's also the danger of getting *two* sore boobs! If I climb into the boat, people on shore or other boaters might see me naked! Even if I do get into the boat, with my luck, the marine patrol will come and check me out. Then I get to thinking—*where is mama shark?* I am in the water, and my tummy and bottom are *fish belly white*. I plead, and Henry finally relents. He tosses me my swimsuit, which I quickly put on. He throws the little snot back, and before it even hits the water, I've rocketed up the ladder and I'm into the boat. Ten minutes later a family anchors fifty yards in front of us. Five minutes after that, a marine patrol boat ties up to them. So that was Gail's Big Adventure (7/16/03).

Pistachio Nut Pudding
By Pat O'Connor

1 box of instant pistachio nut pudding
1 can of crushed pineapple
1 container of regular Cool Whip
1 C. of miniature, colored marshmallows
1 C. of small walnut pieces

Empty the box of pudding into a large bowl. Drain and squeeze the can of pineapple and mix well with the pudding. Fold in the container of Cool Whip. Fold in the marshmallows and walnut pieces. All ingredient amounts are approximate.

Confetti Cheese Ball
By Linda McGee

three 8 oz. pkgs. cream cheese
one 4 oz. jar dried beef
one 4 oz. can chopped olives
one 4 oz. can chopped mushrooms
3 or 4 chopped green onions
3 Tbs. MSG (monosodium glutamate) Accent
1 sm. jar of pimento

Mix all ingredients—form into a ball—chill several hours.

Serve with crackers.

Chinese Chicken Salad

3 cooked chicken breasts or 4 halves (Cook with slice of fresh ginger for 20 minutes. Cool and slice.)

wonton skins sliced and fried (or crisp Chinese noodles)

green leaf lettuce, romaine, iceberg, butter lettuce (Bibb) mixture

6 green onions, sliced

1/4 C. (or less) sesame seeds, toasted

1 small pkg. almonds, toasted

Combine and add dressing before serving.

Dressing:

8 Tbs. sugar

2 tsp. Accent

8 Tbs. cider vinegar

1 tsp. or less pepper

1 C. salad oil

1 tsp. sesame oil

Cook and dissolve over low heat the first four ingredients. Then add oil and refrigerate.

Boater's Tips for Handling Laundry at Sea:
Issue each person two towels in his color—one for freshwater bathing and one for saltwater bathing. With clothespins or spring clamps, hang up the freshwater towels on one side of the boat and saltwater towels on the other side of the boat to dry. When it's time to wash them, once a week or so, put the dirty laundry in a sealable drum or a five-gallon bucket with a Gamma seal (a top that spins on and off), along with detergent and water, and put it in the bilge or somewhere out of the way and let the rocking action of the boat do the washing for you! If you rig up a black plastic shower bladder filled with freshwater, people can bathe, rinse, and sit around the deck to air-dry. Saves on towels.

A WWOW boating raft-up.

Overnight or weekend trips to Pigeon Key in the Middle Keys or Flamingo Park in the Everglades National Park are favorite Wild Women activities, and of course they *must* drive their boats like bats out of hell to get there!

Hey, can you see what's inside this tube?

Splat! It's water, silly!

WWOW member Pat O'Connor and Kathy "Fang" Donovan on their way from a Wild Women on the Water weekend at Pigeon Key.

A NAUTICAL SAGA ON FLORIDA BAY
(A true adventure on the water)
By Pat O'Connor

After departing Bayside Marina in Key Largo and heading out into Florida Bay in my trusty boat, *Where-Am-I*, with Mate Ritz LeFebvre, en route to the WWOW weekend outing on Pigeon Key, we were pressed into a life-saving mission.

As we were a mile or so from Tavernier Creek to meet other WWOWs, we came upon a young couple who had spent the night clinging to an over-turned Hobie Cat and almost in the state of panic. They couldn't get into the boat fast enough, and we completed the rescue and returned them to dry land, at the cost of one pair of reading glasses.

The remainder of the trip was without any other incident, even though I had to play "follow the leader" because I didn't have my seeing-eye dog.

The weekend was very enjoyable and the hi-lite [*sic*] of my winter in Key Largo and I am looking forward to the activities of next winter.

Pat Where-Am-I

Scenes from Pigeon Key

Pigeon Key tram.

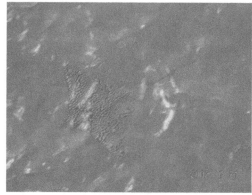

Spotted eagle ray.

All this is mine for the weekend?

Waiting for the others.

Ham

Buy the cheapest.
Bake 2 hours at 300 degrees, without glazing
Glaze:
1½ C. brown sugar
1 C. orange marmalade
1 C. Dijon
Cloves

Cover the ham with the glaze, insert cloves into the skin, and bake the ham for 1½ hours at 350 degrees.

Whipped Potatoes

5 lb. cooked mashed potatoes
1 stick of margarine
2 lb. of sour cream
chives
salt and white pepper

Whip together potatoes and margarine. Cut up chives, and sprinkle them, along with salt and pepper onto the potatoes. Stir in sour cream. Put in a casserole dish and bake at 350 degrees until a crust forms on the top.

Stringy Bread

1 loaf French bread
1 C. mozzarella cheese, shredded
3 oz. cream cheese, softened
2 Tbs. butter or margarine, softened
1/4 C. green onions with green tops, chopped
1/2 tsp. garlic salt

Mix cheeses, butter, garlic salt, and chopped green onions. Slice a loaf of French bread almost through (like you do for garlic bread). Spread some of cheese mixture on each slice.

Wrap in aluminum foil (double layer if doing on grill.)

Bake at 350 degrees for about 20–30 minutes (until cheese mix is melted) or place on barbeque for about 10 minutes, turning once.

World's Best Key Lime Pie
By Tanya Feddern-Bekcan

Equipment:

sharp knife to cut the Key limes

cutting board to cut the Key limes on

lemon or lime squeezer

a cup to squeeze the Key lime juice into

1/4 C. measure

1/2 C. measure

teaspoon

tablespoon

can opener

large stainless steel bowl

electric mixer, preferably with stainless steel mixer blades

small spatula or large silverware tablespoon (preferred)

Pie shell: graham cracker crust. (I use store bought.)

Filling:

one 14 oz. can of Eagle Brand sweetened condensed milk

1/4–1/2 C. of fresh Key lime juice (I like it tart, so I use 1/2 C.)

3 egg yolks (save the egg whites for later)

Add all the ingredients together and beat with the electric beater on medium speed until it becomes thick. Pour into a graham cracker pie shell.

Topping, meringue:
3 egg whites
6 Tbs. sugar
1 tsp. of vanilla

To ensure a flawless meringue, make sure to thoroughly clean your electric beater before continuing. Pour the egg whites and vanilla into the large stainless steel bowl. Beat the egg whites with the electric beater on high until you can form stiff peaks in the meringue. Add the sugar gradually to the meringue while still mixing the meringue with the mixer. Spread on top of the pie with smooth strokes of a small spatula or silver tablespoon. You can create small peaks on top of the meringue by pressing lightly down with the spoon and lifting up—a small peak should form on the meringue as it tries to cling to the spoon. Preheat the oven to 350 degrees. Cook for about 15 minutes or until the meringue is a pale honey color. (The peaks on the meringue may be a darker brown.) Let cool before eating.

(**Note:** the slightest fleck of grease or yolk will prevent meringue from forming properly. For those reasons, don't use plastic bowls, and separate each egg in a small bowl first before adding it to the rest—just in case. Also, fresh, cold eggs separate easier, but for making meringue, eggs whites work best if they're at room temperature and three or four days old.)

HOW RAPISTS TARGET THEIR VICTIMS

Convicted rapists offered up these insights as to how and why they chose their women victims:

- They like women with long hair because it gives them something to grab onto, to more easily control their victim.
- Whether or not women incite rapists' lust by wearing "provocative" clothing is a moot point.
- The fact is rapists look for easy prey where the clothes don't get in the way. They want to remove her clothes quickly, do "it," and get away as fast as possible. They might use scissors or knife to cut away clothes they can't quickly pull off.
- Believe it or not, you are most apt to be raped between five and eight o'clock in the morning at a convenience store or super-market parking lot.
- They sneak up on someone who is dis-tracted. Don't be pawing through your

purse, reading ads or newspaper, magazine, etc., or talking on your cell phone while you are walking, or sitting inside your car with the engine off and the doors unlocked.

- Be aware of your surroundings. Ask a security guard or someone else to go with you if you feel uneasy.

- Besides parking lots of grocery stores and offices and parking garages, rapists lurk behind buildings, in alleys, and inside public restrooms. Don't take the stairwell, even though it's good exercise—it's just too isolated. Wait for the next elevator if a suspicious-looking man gets on.

- They usually take their victims to another, more secluded place where they can rape without interruption.

- Even if he has a gun, ***do not get into that car!*** If he's armed, scream, break away, and run away from him at a zigzag. If you are in your car, don't be afraid to run over him! Better to be shot or raped where you are than to be raped in a remote area, where he might also torture or murder you. In a remote area your body might never be found to give your loved ones closure.

- Chances are, he *won't* have a gun, because ordinary rape is only a three- to five-year sentence, whereas *armed* rape is a much stiffer penalty of fifteen to twenty years.
- Don't make it easy for him. If you seem too tough, he'll leave you alone and look for a more susceptible victim.
- Put up a fight! Women fight dirty, so it's OK to bite, kick, scratch, pull hair, jab, and pinch! Of course, you have a better chance of winning if, beforehand, you've already studied a good self-defense video. Go for his vulnerable areas: like continuously push your finger against the hollow at the base of his throat; gouge his eyes; drive the heel of your hand up his nose; pinch hard his upper inner thigh or between armpit and elbow in the soft flesh under his arm; slam sides of the knees; bend fingers and elbows the wrong way; or stomp on his feet; there is much more you can do than just kneeing or kicking his groin.
- Let him see that you are not so vulnerable because you are carrying something in your hands that will make him keep his distance, like an umbrella, a Taser, or pepper spray.

- Scream and holler "Stay back!" or "Stop!" At the same time push your hands in his direction.

If you find yourself in close proximity to someone who makes you feel uncomfortable, try to defuse the situation by looking him in the eye and making friendly small talk. By doing so, you are humanizing both you and him. (But don't fool yourself in the process into thinking he's an OK guy and letting your guard down; listen to your inner woman—she is trying to warn and protect you!) Many rapists have poor self-esteem. They feel cast out by society, which makes them angry, so they retaliate by attacking the weakest, most vulnerable members of society—women and children—in order to make themselves feel strong and powerful. By being a nice person talking politely to him you are giving him the benefit of a doubt, you are accepting him (at least superficially) as a regular person, and you become less of an object for his hostility. He knows you've gotten a good look at him and can describe him to the police, so he just might change his mind about pulling any "funny stuff" with you. One old lady sitting at a bus stop sensed that she was about to be mugged by a young man creeping up behind her.

She turned around, smiled, and said, "Hello! Don't I know your mother? What's your name again?" Her would-be attacker ducked his head, muttered something, and slunk off.

Always pay attention to your woman's intuition! It's much better to be embarrassed than to be dead. Unfortunately, too many women die, but never from embarrassment.

Important Note: After writing this, I have since seen the DVD video *Kid Escape! from Child Abductors*, and downloaded and read the free CD and book that comes with it, *Self-Defense Secrets for Moms*. Both are by John Hall. They take an entirely *different approach*, a life-saving approach that makes much more sense to those of us (like myself!) who can't do much with martial arts. I *highly* recommend it! Visit his website, KidsEscape.org. You can purchase these vitally important educational materials by e-mailing him at JohnHall@KidEscape.org or calling him at 1 (800) 486-1939.

Life-Saving Tip: If someone tries to strangle you—simply *throw up your arms straight up next to your ears and twirl around,* **screaming!** Your arms will automatically dislodge his hands from your neck. Other ways: If he's facing you, make a wedge with your hands and arms and, from underneath, quickly thrust up between his arms, forcing them apart. Or twist one of his fingers back, like his little finger, to cause him pain so he'll release.

Another Tip: *Use mechanical advantage whenever and wherever you can.* Go for the opening. Twist your body to press against the weakest part of his grasp or drop down and out. The hand is weak without its thumb, so if he grabs your arm or leg, peel off his thumb and pull your limb away. If he grabs you by the hair, pin his hand to your head with both of your hands, take control of his hand, turn around and twist his hand towards the outside of his elbow. Now you have control of him, and he is the one who is hurting!

Vegetable Casserole
By Gail Feddern

*Optional—sliced tomatoes, carrots, celery, other vegetables

(Can add a drained can of salmon, tuna, or cooked poultry to make it a complete main meal)

Swanson's chicken broth – use in cooking vegetables in place of water

1 head of cauliflower

4 bell peppers—red, green, yellow, orange

1 or 2 yellow crook neck summer squash

*1/2 can of pumpkin

1 piece of calabaza or winter squash

1 medium large onion

1 egg

1/8 C. liquid margarine spray

1/8 C. fat-free half and half cream (I prefer Land O' Lakes brand)

1 or 1½ sleeve of Ritz or Townhouse crackers, divided

*Hungry Jack potato flakes

1 bag of shredded cheese, divided

Pam cooking spray

*Parmesan cheese, grated

Salt and pepper or other seasoning, like 1/2 packet of Badia tropical (orange box)

Thinly slice onion. Medium slice the summer squash. Chop winter squash into 1/2-inch pieces. Starting with winter squash, sauté these three ingredients and optional vegetables in a Pam-sprayed pan; add broth as needed. Prepare cauliflower and cook until soft. Mash it up, put it in a bowl, and stir in egg and liquids. Mince bell peppers and add to sautéed vegetables and cover. Line a Pam sprayed casserole baking dish with crackers. Combine most of the shredded cheese with all vegetables and rest of ingredients and pour into dish. Crush the rest of the crackers and sprinkle, along with remaining shredded cheese, over top. Shake Parmesan cheese over top. Bake in oven at 450 degrees for 15 minutes.

A Life-Saving Tip: *If you get a cramp in your leg while swimming or snorkeling, press hard on your upper lip.* Maintain the pressure, and after two to three minutes, the cramp will go away. You can do this even with a snorkel in your mouth. In fact, if you are wearing a mask and snorkel, keep them on your face and don't panic.

Note: Cramps are caused by pockets of calcium lactate in the muscle. Personally, I've noticed that if I take calcium or ingest a high-calcium food or milk late at night, I am likely to be awakened by a cramp in my foot (especially if the room is cold), so I have to get out of bed and roll the bottom of my foot on a bottle to alleviate the pain. Perhaps drinking milk can cause a cramp during exercise, and that is the reason our mothers warned us about swimming too soon after eating.

Another Life-Saving Tip: *If you get caught in an undertow,* don't exhaust yourself by trying to swim against the current. Instead, *swim* **parallel** *to the shore* until you get out of the current and can swim back to shore.

Gail's Mom Celia's Swiss Steak Recipe
By Gail Feddern

1½ lb. round steak, about 3/4 inches thick
salt
pepper
flour
4 Tbs. shortening
2 medium onions, sliced
1 large can of tomatoes, with liquid
1 tsp. sugar
1/2 tsp. thyme
1/2 tsp. marjoram

Pound the salt, pepper, and flour into the steak. Brown it in a pan with shortening. Turn off the heat. Cover the steak with sliced onions and pour a whole can of tomatoes over it. Sprinkle sugar, thyme, and marjoram over all. Cook on medium for 5 minutes, or until mixture starts bubbling. Stir, cover, and simmer for 1 hour. Check frequently to guard against burning. Serves 5.

Chinese Stew
(A hurricane meal)
By Gail Feddern

1 pkg. Nissin Original Chow Mein Teriyaki beef flavor dinner ($1 at Family Dollar Store)

1 pkg. Nissin Top Ramen Oodles of Noodles beef flavor soup ($1 for a six-pack at Family Dollar Store)

one 12 oz. can of Hormel Roast Beef with gravy (sold at Walgreen's)

1 pkg. frozen peas (preferred), cooked, or 1 can of peas, drained

Prepare each separately according to directions. Mix all together and serve. ***This is a quick, good, and cheap meal!*** Takes 10–15 minutes or less to make. Serves 4.

Helpful Household Hint: **Stab a cardboard package of frozen vegetables five or six times with a fork, or once with a knife, and throw it in the microwave on full power for five minutes.** Saves on time and dirty dishes.

Six-Minute Split-Pea Soup
(A pressure cooker meal; can be a hurricane meal)

By Gail Feddern

1 lb. pkg. of dried split peas

6–8 C. of water

ham hock or 1/2 lb. canned ham, cubed, or 3 bacon strips plus a packet of ham bouillon

1 large onion, chopped, or 1 rounded Tbs. of dried onion flakes

2 carrots, peeled and sliced, or dehydrated vegetable flakes

2 sticks of celery, sliced, or 1 tsp. celery salt, or dry veggie flakes

a pinch of thyme

1 large bay leaf

2 bouillon cubes (ham, chicken, or beef)

salt to taste

garlic powder or buds to taste (optional)

Sort and rinse the dried peas. Combine all ingredients in a pressure cooker. Note: if you're in a hurry, instead of slicing and chopping the fresh vegetables, you can use your food processor. I like my hand-crank two-cup mini-food processor from Amazon for this because it's so easy to clean, and being nonelectric, it works even after a hurricane. Set your pressure cooker on the delicate setting (if it has that option). Under high heat, pressurize the pressure cooker; after it begins to puff steam, cook for 6 minutes. Turn it off and let the pressure drop naturally. Remove the lid. Remove the bay leaf. Stir and serve.

One-Minute Pea Soup

1 can of peas (no-salt variety is healthier)
1 packet of ham bouillon
4 oz. of low-fat cottage cheese (increases the protein; optional)

Open the can of peas and pour all its contents into a blender. Add the packet of ham bouillon, and if desired, the cheese. Blend until smooth. Pour into a bowl and heat in the microwave for approximately 1 minute or until hot enough to suit you.

A reminder that *your diamond ring will cut glass*. Scratch or score the glass surface or mirror if it's *vitally* important to leave a message, and you have no other means; remember, it *is* permanent! You can incise a circle or square, cover the area with a piece of cloth to protect yourself from glass shards, gently tap, and that section of glass will pop out, leaving a hole. So if you ever get trapped in a glass elevator or whatever. . .

Another reminder—that interior walls of a building are usually made of drywall, which means that if you find yourself imprisoned in a bedroom, apartment, or even an office, you can probably *bash or kick your way out.*

Do-It-Themselves Omelets
By Camping Queen Judy O'Hara Vetrick

This is the ideal setup for making breakfast for a bunch of people when you are camping.

> a large boiling pot of water (Judy uses an outdoor turkey fryer outfit powered by propane gas.)
> slotted ladle or long-handled tongs
> quart-size Ziploc freezer bags
> permanent felt-tip marker or ball-point pen
> a picnic table or card table
> a garbage bag attached to the end of the table by clamps or other means
> a box of eggs
> chopped vegetables that are normal choices for omelets, such as onions, bell peppers, mushrooms, tomatoes, spinach, etc.
> shredded cheeses
> chopped ham or sausage
> salt and pepper

Lay out the vegetables and meats, cheeses, and condiments on the table. Place the box of eggs near the garbage bag. Put the Ziploc bags at either end of the table. Let each person take a Ziploc bag, write their name or initials on it, and put eggs and his or her choices of other ingredients into the bag. It works best if they don't fill the bag more than 1/4 full. With your fingers, squish the outside of the bag to mix the contents. Fold over once to press the air out, and zip it closed. Drop the bag into the boiling water and cook for exactly 9 minutes. When it's done, fish it out, pour it onto a plate, and eat it. At our WWOW camp each woman was responsible for her own plate and wash-up afterward at our dishwashing station, but you can use disposable tableware, instead.

**Above: At last! Judy finds a man who will listen.
Mr. Stud is an excellent conversationalist.
Maybe that's why he's so popular?
Below: Bonfire cooking at our fall
camping trips tastes great!**

**A whale shark is an amazing fish story, even
for a WWOW fishing tournament.**

**Helpful Hint for Cleaning Dolphin (Mahi-
Mahi/Dorado):** With the point of your knife, cut
around the perimeter of the fillet you want to make
but not underneath it yet. Next, slit the skin lengthwise down the center, down to the bone. Now, go
back and cut underneath the outside edges and
remove two fillets from one side. Then turn each
fillet over and cut away and discard the bloodline.
For the last step, slide your blade between the skin
and the flesh. (Skin side is down, against the table.)
You will find it much easier processing two narrow

fillets than one large one. Flip the fish over and repeat procedure on other side.

Note: Try using a Chinese cleaver to clean fish instead of a fillet knife.

Cabbage Salad
By Daryl Stone

In a large bowl, place the following:
1 head of cabbage, chopped
1 onion, chopped
1/2 C. sugar

Mix together the above ingredients and let stand while you combine the remaining ingredients in a sauce pan.

1 tsp. sugar
1/2 tsp. salt
1/2 tsp. dry mustard
1/2 tsp. celery seed
1/2 C. oil
1/2 C. vinegar

Bring these ingredients to a boil. Pour over cabbage mixture. Let stand.

Spinach Soufflé
By Daryl Stone

2 pkgs. frozen spinach, cooked and drained.
2 eggs
1¾ C. milk
1 tsp. salt
2/3 C. bread crumbs
1½ C. provolone cheese, shredded

Beat eggs, milk, and salt. Stir in spinach, bread crumbs, and half of the cheese. Pour into a 1½ qt. buttered baking dish. Top with the rest of the cheese and sprinkle with paprika. Bake 35 minutes at 375 degrees.

Spinach Salad
By Daryl Stone

1 large bag of spinach (1 lb.)
1/2 head of lettuce or leaf lettuce, chopped
1 C. bean sprouts, rinsed and drained
1 C. sliced water chestnuts
3 hard-boiled eggs, sliced
10 strips of bacon, fried crisp and crumbled

Mix above ingredients together.

Dressing:
3/4 C. sugar
2 tsp. Worcestershire sauce
1/4 C. wine vinegar
1/4 C. Wesson oil
1/3 C. catsup
1 small onion, chopped

Blend these ingredients in a blender and refrigerate.

Toss the spinach salad with the dressing and serve.

Crab Rangoon
By Daryl Stone

8 oz. can of crabmeat, drained
8 oz. pkg. cream cheese, softened
1/4 tsp. garlic powder
1/2 tsp. steak sauce
16 oz. pkg. wonton wrappers
oil for frying

Combine crabmeat, cream cheese, garlic powder, and steak sauce. Put 1/2 tsp. of mixture in center of each wrapper as directed on package. Deep fry until delicately browned. Makes five dozen.

Catching crawfish is a favorite pastime with Keys people.

Crawfish or Florida spiny lobster season attracts thousands of visitors to the Keys, making competition tough but boosting the summer tourist dollars. As of this writing, the limit is six lobsters per person per day. The sport season is the last Wednesday and Thursday of July, and the regular lobster season is August 6 through March 31. Crawfish must have carapaces longer than three inches. You must have a lobster gauge/ruler and measure it underwater when you catch it. Certain areas are off-limits. You want to understand the laws correctly and not disobey them. So be sure to verify with the authorities *every year* that there have been no changes.

During the season, you can buy crawfish kits just about anywhere. The best way to use them is to position your net perpendicular to the rock or coral head that the lobsters are hiding under. (Don't let the lobster see it.) You don't want the net bag flat against the bottom; you want one side of the rim resting against the bottom. With your tickle stick, reach into the hole and tickle the tail of the biggest lobster. When he shoots backward out of the hole and into the net, flip the net with a quick flick of the wrist so that he's caught in the bag of the net. Pin him down with one hand while you measure him with the lobster gauge. If the three-inch gap on the gauge slips past the lobster's carapace, then he's too short, and you must let him go. If he's a keeper, hold him securely and put him in your bug bag and latch it. Watch out that he doesn't gore your knuckles with his horns, or suddenly flip away while you are trying to get him into the bag.

I think twice before putting my hand into a hole because there might be a moray or a crab in there. Look first to see if there is a moray there. If no moray is visible, then slide your hand underneath the lobster, palm up, along the bottom, so that you can grab the base of the lobster's antennae. The reason for the hand along the bottom is that it avoids the antenna's spines, which prevent the hand from reaching the base of the antenna, and a moray has difficulty biting a hand that is against the bottom. The base segments of the antennae do not break easily. Squeeze the antennae together and pull the lobster out of the hole. If you touch something slimy, then pull your hand out quickly—it might be a moray.

During lobster season, most crawfish will be found inshore. Like people, they get naked to have sex, and they like to honeymoon in the Keys. Yes, they must shed their shells before mating. If you find a soft "rubber lobster," it has probably already mated and is waiting for its new, larger shell to harden. (They also shed their shells and grow new ones if they lose a part, like a leg or an antenna.) Crawfish out on the reef tend to have eggs/berries attached to the undersides of their tails. It is illegal for you to take those lobsters or to remove the "berries"! Don't try it. Female lobsters have tremendous maternal instincts, and many will let themselves be torn in half rather than come out of a hole. Leave them alone to repopulate the supply.

When you catch Florida crawfish, put them in a mesh "bug bag," dip them often in seawater, and keep them in the shade. As with all shellfish, you want to keep them alive.

When you get them home, you need to prepare them for dinner or the freezer. Put on your gloves, pick one up by the thorax in one hand, and with the other hand tuck the tail up under itself, and wring the tail off by twisting your hands in opposite directions. The only part really worth eating is the tail. It's not necessary, but if you want, you can remove the gut. Break off an antenna and trim away the flexible part. Insert the tip into the anus at the end of the tail (a hole-slit in front of the tail fins). Push the antenna in further, twist several times to wind the intestine around it, and carefully withdraw it. If you want to freeze lobster tails, freeze them raw; they'll keep better than if they're cooked.

Lobster Salad
By Gail Feddern

4 Florida lobster tails
4 eggs
2–4 scallions
Hellman's Blue Ribbon mayonnaise
stuffed olives
capers (optional)
celery (optional)
lettuce (optional)
salt
bay leaf or crab boil
paprika

Bring a pot of water with 1 tsp. of salt and a bay leaf or crab boil to a rolling boil. Add lobster tails. Bring to a boil again and cook for approximately 10 minutes. Remove tails from water and let cool.

Boil the eggs. (I like an egg cooker for this.)

While the lobsters and eggs are boiling and cooling, chop the scallions into 1/4inch pieces. Chop the celery into 1/4 inch pieces.

When the lobsters are cool enough, crack the tail shells by squeezing them with your hands or use a knife to remove the meat. Cut the meat into 1/2- or 1-inch pieces. If you want to serve lobster salad right away, cool the hard-boiled eggs and lobster meat quickly by placing them in bowl(s) in the freezer for a few minutes.

When these main ingredients are cold, proceed with making the salad. Chop the hard-boiled eggs into 1/4-inch pieces. Get a medium large bowl and combine eggs, lobster chunks, stuffed olives, scallions, and celery and capers if desired. Mix in enough mayonnaise. Serve on beds of lettuce leaves. Sprinkle paprika on top of the mixture. Makes 4 servings.

Helpful Household Hint: Keep scallions fresh by putting them in a glass of water. Place it on a windowsill. The scallions will grow roots. You can then harvest just what you need, and you don't have to throw any away because they're all dried out. They should last indefinitely as long as you keep changing the water and occasionally add a few drops of liquid fertilizer.

To preserve scallions that you use for cooking, it's OK to freeze them. Rinse and trim the bunch. With a pair of scissors, snip them to pieces into a Ziploc freezer bag and freeze them.

Lobster Fiesta
By Gail Feddern

2 cooked lobster tails, cut up

2 large potatoes, cut up

3 medium large onions, cut up

2 cloves garlic

1/2 medium small green bell pepper, cut up

1/2 medium small red bell pepper, cut up

Salt, pepper, and seasoned salt

1/2 stick (4 Tbs.) margarine or butter

3 Tbs. lemon or lime juice (or juice of 1 Key lime)

corn kernels, cheese, dash Tabasco, stuffed olives, cut-up scallions

In a large iron skillet, brown lobster in margarine or butter. Sprinkle with lemon juice and set aside. Cook potatoes, onions, and garlic; when almost done, add peppers and cook until done. Add rest of ingredients and serve with dash of Tabasco sauce. Serves 2.

DIVING THE BRIDGES

You probably know that the Florida Keys came into existence as a community when Henry Flagler built his overseas railroad. Marathon, located in the middle of the chain of islands on Vaca Key, was the supply depot and staging area. The railroad was destroyed in the infamous hurricane of 1935, which killed five hundred people. Instead of rebuilding the railroad, the state of Florida bought it for $640,000 and built a road to replace it, using the old railroad bed. Paralleling today's US-1 (a.k.a. Overseas Highway), the Old Road can be found on many of the Keys. Local Keys residents often bypass traffic jams by taking the Old Road. (Recently, the local government installed a series of stop signs to discourage this.) US-1 was modernized in the 1980's, making it four-lanes in many places, and building new bridges near some of the old railway bridges. You are allowed to fish off many of the old bridges, or what's left of them.

Some people, my husband and I included, like to dive in the channels and around the bridge pilings. The water depth is about fifteen feet. Some people free-dive or snorkel from the nearest point of land. I would discourage this because it's very dangerous. A lot of boats go through the channels, and you risk getting run over and cut up by a propeller. It's safest to scuba dive because when you hear a boat coming, you can, and should, hug the bottom while it passes over you.

Important: Do not attempt to scuba dive unless you've taken a course and are certified! Any dive shop will be happy to teach you for a fee. If you let a friend "show you how", you could end up dead.

The other thing that makes it so dangerous is that you can only dive during slack high tide or slack low tide. The slack periods vary and may only be fifteen minutes or less before the tide changes direction and the current starts ripping through too strongly for you to swim against.

If you get caught and you are without scuba, swim over to the land or to the nearest bridge piling closer to land. Aim for the piling's downstream side and get behind it and rest. Then swim and claw your way to the upstream side. The current will plaster you against it, but stay in the center and avoid letting the current rip you away. After you get your breath, swim like crazy at an angle into the current toward the next piling that's in the direction of the closest land. Depending on the angle, how hard you can swim, and how fast the current is, you will end up (ideally) at the upstream side of the next piling. If you end up at the downstream side, then repeat the previous actions from the last piling, using vectoring tactics to finally get yourself safely back to land. If this is beyond your capabilities, then find something to hang onto until you can flag down a passing boater. An alternative is to swim directly toward land. You will end up downstream of the land, but will land safely on the mud flats that parallel the channels, where you can wave for someone to pick you up. Boating traffic is heavy during lobster season. Pray you get rescued and not run over.

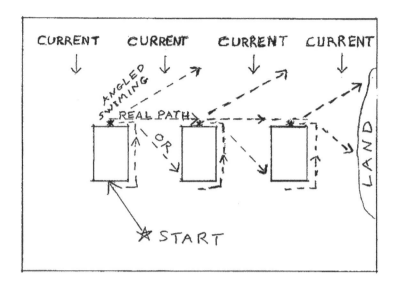

If you are scuba diving and run out of air, you can try the above strategy, but it will be much more difficult because your gear will cause a lot of drag. Yes, you can ditch it. But if it were me, I would look for something to hang onto behind a bridge piling and wait for some boat to pick me up. There are barnacles and ropes and debris and maybe a grounding rod for lightning.

But if you are a savvy diver, you won't let yourself get in such a position in the first place. Plan your dive before you go. Scuba dive from a boat. Things to consider are current, wind, and the position of the boat and your own position relative to all three. Anchor your boat in such a manner so that it won't bang against a bridge piling or anything else, even when the current reverses direction. If possible, leave someone on the boat who knows how to operate it so they can pick you up if need be.

Some of the bridges' supports are round columns, some square, some rectangular, and the old Flagler railroad bridges have arches for the boats to go through. Regardless, your technique remains basically the same if you are stranded and need to get out of the current and take yourself back to land.

This is one instance where a dive knife might actually prove useful because there is a lot of junk under the bridges, especially ropes and fishing lines, and it might be helpful to cut yourself free if you get tangled up. Who knows? You might find a nice anchor down there to salvage. If so, you could cut the line to a manageable length and tie it to your boat's anchor line, to be pulled up later when you're back in the boat.

We are working divers, so we have a couple of three-foot ropes or bungee cords with snap swivels, attached to the starboard gunnel near the stern, with the swivels a couple of feet below the water surface. When we return to the boat, we hook our goody bags to the swivels before we get in the boat. I have a bad back and can't get into the boat with all my gear on, so I hook it on one of the swivels. I also grab one to hang on to when I jump into a current so I won't be swept away while my husband hands me my gear. Normally, we float a knotted safety line tied around a boat cushion in a goodly current—if we were out on the reef—but bridge areas are too congested, making a safety line more hazardous than safe.

Current is almost always less on the bottom than on the surface, so take advantage of that fact whenever you can. This is not a deep dive, so if you want to wait for your buddy, don't hang on the top of the anchor rope, where you'll get beat up by the current; meet him on the bottom at the anchor, instead. Actually, the murky water under bridges is not very conducive for diving with a buddy, so don't worry if you get separated. As soon as you go in the water, head for the bottom. If the current is very strong, go down the anchor rope, clearing your ears as you go. (In such cases, I like to bring along a two-pronged grappling hook to claw my way upstream, using the manmade junk on the bottom to pull against.)

If the current is so strong that it displaces your facemask, abort the dive! Just get back in the boat and wait for the slack. If you missed it, give up and go home. Try again another day.

But if everything is OK, head upstream. You always want to be upstream of the boat. When you reach your first bridge piling, come up on the lee side to verify your position. Where is your boat? How many pilings between you and the one closest to your boat? As you dive the bottom, always keep track of where you are by counting pilings. When your pressure gauge reads 1,500 lb., come up and check your position again, using the same procedure. Repeat at 1,000 lb., and start working your way over toward your boat's anchor. After the slack, when you feel the current starting again, but in the opposite direction, get directly ahead of your boat. At 500 lb., surface and let the current carry you straight back to your boat. Bang your hand against the side of the boat so your buddies onboard will know you've arrived and can assist you.

Two major rules for scuba diving: (1) *Never* hold your breath on ascent! (2) Don't panic.

Warning! *If skin-diving or snorkeling, refuse any offers of air from a scuba diver on the bottom.* That's compressed air and it can give you an air embolism! One year someone died that way. The snorkeler took in a lungful of compressed air from his scuba-equipped buddy on the bottom and rose. The air from the scuba tank expanded in his lungs the higher he went in the water column (less atmospheric pressure—gases expand), he probably didn't even exhale on the way up, and by the time he reached the surface, his lungs ruptured and he died.

Another Warning: You should probably stay away from the Channel Five Bridge. It's shallower there, and there is not much to see anyway. Beware! It's the lair of **Charlie the Rapin' Turtle**. (He put the *terr* and *rapin* in *terrapin!*) Yes, there resides a huge, horny loggerhead turtle. And he's homosexual. He's already raped a few men. He has a predilection for men in pink bikini bathing suits. One man got raped twice! (I think he must be the one wearing the pink bikini.) You would think the man would have known better than to come back a second time. I guess either he couldn't believe it, or he was stubborn—or maybe he liked it! Nobody knows where Charlie came from, perhaps Key West. I don't know if he's still lurking underneath Channel Five Bridge or not. Understandably, some victims are reluctant to report their rapes. Some of Charlie's early rapes were reported anonymously, coming forth only after the guy in the pink bikini admitted assault to his body by a reptile. I haven't heard of any incidents recently. Perhaps Charlie swam back to Key West. But I'm not making this stuff up, folks! Sea turtle rape was written up in the local papers several years ago.

Why would a sea turtle commit an unnatural act like rape? I don't know. Perhaps his perversion came about from eating used condoms from sewage outfall. Key West does have a centralized sewage treatment plant (and soon Key Largo will have one), and when there is too much rain, well, don't the flood gates have to open? Sea turtles are attracted to condoms and balloons because they resemble jellyfish, which turtles like to eat. All that stuff inside could affect turtles. Could have Super-Sexed Charlie.

How is the diver-victim at risk? Well, so far they've all been men, so at least they don't have to worry about pregnancy. Well, not that a sea turtle could impregnate a woman diver, anyway. Hmm, where did Teenage Mutant Ninja Turtles come from?

I don't know if Charlie's rape victims are at risk for HIV (Mr. Pink Bikini should definitely get himself checked), but turtles *do* carry salmonella and human papilloma virus. But most of all, **unless**

he's wearing a scuba tank, a diver being pinned to the bottom by an amorous sea turtle is at risk of being *drowned!* Because Charlie takes ten minutes to climax.

There is something very repellant about being raped by a reptile.

It's bad enough when you get molested by a marine mammal. But at least the places where you can swim with the dolphins (porpoises, *not* mahi-mahi) warn you beforehand that if a male dolphin takes a shine to you he might rub his penis against the inside of your knee. I believe you might have to sign a written release before they let you in the water. Besides, they're not going to let you drown.

Spinach-Stuffed Chicken Breast with Yogurt Sauce

By Daryl Stone

4 chicken breasts halves, boned with skin on

2 Tbs. olive oil, divided

1 medium onion, chopped

1 lb. fresh spinach, washed, drained, and chopped

1/2 C. skim milk ricotta cheese

1/4 C. grated Parmesan cheese

1 tsp. dried basil, crushed, or 1 Tbs. fresh basil, chopped

1 Tbs. lemon juice

1 tsp. dried thyme

1 tsp. no-salt seasoning, such as Mrs. Dash

Loosen skin of chicken breasts by slipping a finger between the flesh and the skin, but leave the skin attached on one side. Cut away the fat and set aside.

Prepare stuffing:

Sauté onion in 1 Tbs. olive oil, add spinach, and cook, stirring until spinach is wilted. Let spinach

96

cool, then add ricotta, Parmesan, and basil. Stuff each chicken breast between flesh and skin with a fourth of the mixture. Place skin side up in a baking dish. Brush with additional 1 Tbs. olive oil, then sprinkle on lemon juice, thyme, and seasoning. Bake 45 minutes at 375 degrees or until the skin is golden brown.

Yogurt Sauce:
1 C. plain low-fat yogurt
1 Tbs. red wine vinegar
1 tsp. no-salt seasoning
1 fresh tomato, seeded and chopped

Combine all ingredients and serve at room temperature with chicken.

Key Lime Cake
By Louise Scott

1 pkg. lemon cake mix
1 pkg. lemon instant pudding mix
1 C. water
4 eggs
1 C. salad oil
3 Tbs. Key lime juice

Put all ingredients in mixing bowl and blend with mixer approximately 2 minutes, scraping down sides until mixture is smooth. Beat well. Pour into a greased 13×9-inch pan. Bake 45–60 minutes at 325 degrees. Remove from oven and let stand 10 minutes. Prick surface with fork.

Glaze:
2 C. powdered sugar
1/3 C. lime juice

Combine sugar and juice. Pour glaze mixture over cake.
Serve and enjoy.

Cowboy Caviar
By Cindy Strack

1 can black beans
1 can corn
green pepper, diced
red pepper, diced
green onions, chopped
feta cheese
Tostitos
1/3 C. sugar
1/3 C. vinegar
1/3 C. olive oil

Combine all. Serve with scoop Tostitos.

**Wild Women on the Water celebrates its birthdays
by indulging its sweet-tooth.**

Ritzy Casserole
By Gail Feddern

This is a great, tasty way to deal with holiday leftovers!

1 can French green beans, drained (or leftover
    green bean casserole)
leftover cooked chicken or turkey, diced
1 C. chicken gravy
ranch dressing
1 sleeve of Ritz crackers
1 Tbs. butter, divided
grated Parmesan or other cheese

Preheat oven to 350 degrees. Mix enough ranch dressing into the gravy to suit your taste. Combine it with the chicken and French beans. Spray an 8¼-inch casserole dish with Pam. Line dish with layer of Ritz crackers. Cover with half the mixture. Dot with pieces of butter. Lay down another layer of Ritz crackers. Cover with rest of mixture. Dot with remaining butter. Crumble remaining Ritz crackers and sprinkle on top. Shake grated cheese generously on top. Bake in center of oven at 350 degrees for fifteen minutes

So-Easy Moon Peanut Butter Bar
By Peggy Moon

1/2 C. peanut butter
1/2 C. butter
1½ C. sugar
2 eggs
1½ tsp. baking power
1/2 tsp. salt
1 tsp. vanilla
1 C. flour

Preheat oven at 350 degrees. Grease and flour a 9×13×2-inch pan.

Melt the peanut butter and butter in a double boiler (or a bowl over hot water). Add remaining ingredients. Stir until blended. Pour into baking pan and bake for 25 to 30 minutes. Recipe makes 2 dozen squares.

Spearfishing is the most ecologically sound method of fishing because you know before you shoot at it whether or not it's suitable.

Hook-and-line fishermen don't know what they've got until they've brought it up. They are not restricted as to depth, and often the fish's air bladder will come out of its mouth, and if it's thrown back, it can't get back down to the bottom. It's doomed to float helplessly on the surface unless the fisherman knows to puncture the air bladder. ***Note:* a considerate angler can keep a large diameter hypodermic syringe onboard for this purpose.** Remove the plunger first. Hold the fish belly up, and carefully insert the hypo needle into the air bladder wherever it's coming out, at the anus/vent or the mouth. If there's water in the syringe, you will see air bubbles releasing.

Spearfisher's Tip: Wrap a fish ruler sticker around the barrel of your gun. Fish look 25 percent larger underwater, and this will help you judge size.

If you are a novice, it's good to get the hang of it by practicing on grunts. They are plentiful, good to eat, and legally you can take as many as you want of any size.

Spearfishing requires skill. It's more like hunting than fishing because usually the fish are wary, and one must stalk them by hiding behind coral heads and sneaking up on them. It is an exercise in futility to chase after them because of course they can swim much faster than you!

Basically, all the waters surrounding the Florida Keys of Monroe County are included in the Florida Keys National Marine Sanctuary. Within the FKNMS there are areas where you may and may not spear fish. Off-limits to spearfishing are State and National parks and smaller National marine sanctuaries within FKNMS, and small protected areas, such as SPAs (Sanctuary Preservation Areas) and other discrete no-take zones. These small areas are visibly marked with large yellow buoys. To know where the parks and sanctuaries, and other large protection zones are, you will have to consult nautical charts and use a compass or GPS (Global Positioning System; it uses satellites).

You may lawfully spear fish south of the Long Key bridge. North of that point to the Miami-Dade County line you may not spear fish in State waters. State waters Atlantic side are 3 miles out from the nearest land. State waters bayside (Gulf of Mexico) are 9 miles out from nearest land. It's not measured from US-1 or even shore—it's measured from the closest island or key or point of land.

I usually spear fish around Conch Reef and Alligator Reef, in areas where it is allowed.

Download on your computer or pick up from a dive shop or bait and tackle store, the "Regulations for Spearfishing for Monroe County, Florida including the Florida Keys National Marine Sanctuary." Or contact FWC (Florida Fish and Wildlife Conservation Commission) or NOAA (National Oceanic and Atmospheric Administration). Their websites are: www.myfwc.com and floridakeys.noaa.gov. Before you consider *any* water activity check with them. Rules and regulations are in flux. The authorities are anticipating adding new fish reserve zones and changes to fishery management. It is essential that you know and obey all the rules to avoid big trouble! Other websites that are helpful are diving forums, such as www.spearboard.com.

Yogurt Chicken

(A Crock-Pot recipe)
By Gail Feddern

1 frying chicken

adobo seasoning

salt and pepper

1 can Campbell's concentrated cream of mushroom soup (low-fat) or cream of chicken soup (low-fat)

16 oz. plain yogurt (low-fat) or sour cream (low-fat)

2 Tbs. butter

1 can evaporated skim milk

6 rounded Tbs. flour

splash of sherry or dry white wine

Season chicken generously with adobo seasoning and lightly with salt and pepper. Place in Crock-Pot. In a bowl, mix soup and yogurt; pour over chicken and sprinkle more adobo seasoning on top. Splash with sherry/wine. Set Crock-Pot to low and cook until done. (Read Crock-Pot instructions.)

Discard bones, cut meat into bite-size pieces, then cover and set aside. Make gravy with remaining ingredients. Combine all. Serve over cooked rice, noodles, or toast. Makes 8 servings.

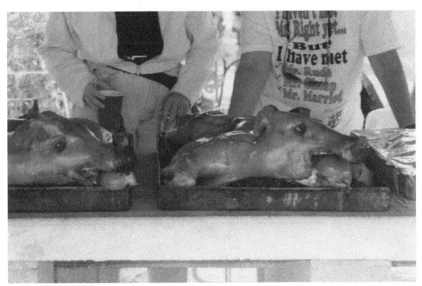

Pigging out at the annual summer WWOW picnic.

Our men are allowed only to the WWOW picnic and the Christmas party.

Except for Mr. Stud, who is *always* welcome.
In fact, you could say his presence is downright mandatory.

WWOW'S MASCOTS

He was our first. The Tool Man came with tool belt and tough attitude in the spring of 2002.
It was at a Flamingo trip that our first
Blow-up doll mascot made his appearance.

His replacement was Mr. Stud, a more sensitive type, but with muscles.

Susie T. was the hostess. To inform the new members, she reminded everybody that we would be going to Flamingo in the Everglades National Park by boat, so "No prom dresses, no high heels, and no guys!" And she backed up her words with flyers. When Pat R.'s significant other, Al, learned of it, he went to an adult store in Marathon and came back with the Tool Man, saying, "She said no guys, but she didn't say no dolls!"

The girls that were *not* members of the trip planning committee had a big surprise for those who were. Their cohorts came by car, making it easy to smuggle things. The attendees came out wearing thrift store prom dresses / bridesmaid dresses, high heels, and tiaras! Pat R. and Cristine P. walked in arm and arm with the Tool Man, dressed in Al's shorts and a WWOW T-shirt. Susie T. and her planners were hysterically surprised.

Alas, Tool Man had no staying power. He must have worn himself out dancing with everybody because the next morning they found him lying on top of a chest of drawers, all deflated except for his most important tool.

Susie T. became the custodian of Tool Man. Then Susie's daughter met him and fell instantly in love, so he went home with her. Here's how they broke up: She forgot she had him in the trunk of her car when she went grocery shopping. Much to her embarrassment, the bag boy nearly dropped the groceries when she popped the trunk and they saw this male vinyl doll collapsed on the floor, except for his screwdriver, which was standing straight up! After that, she took him to her girlfriend's bachelorette party, where it is believed that he eloped with a bridesmaid because he was never seen again.

Later, he was replaced by Mr. Stud—maybe less of a man but a more politically correct figure and a real doll! Mr. Stud went everywhere with the WWOW girls. He went on camping trips (always being careful not to sit too close to the campfire), paddling trips, and picnics; to Flamingo, Nest Key, and Pigeon Key; on boat and yacht rides (but for some reason he was afraid to go fishing with us!); and to parties and sleepovers. When accommodations were such that we had to share two to a bed, we drew straws to see who got to sleep with Mr. Stud, as he was always a good bedfellow and never tossed or turned or hogged the covers.

Many WWOWzers consider him the perfect man. He was always quiet and respectful and a good listener. You could hold his hand and gaze into his eyes and talk to him, and he'd never turn aside (unless a strong breeze came up suddenly). Never a rude sound came out of his mouth. All right, if you sat on him by mistake, sometimes he'd make a rude noise, but it didn't come out of his mouth. He didn't like to be sat on normally.

The Saga of Mr. Stud

Oh, lover!

Mr. Stud and girlfriends.

Mr. Stud drinks a mimosa.

Friends frolicking in the water.

Mr. Stud passes out.

Mr. Stud wants to leave.

Mr. Stud waves good-bye.

Mr. Stud makes a getaway!

Quick! After him, girls!

Alas! Mr. Stud chose to leave us. I guess he got tired of his role reversal of being a one man harem to a hundred wild women. He yearned to be free. One minute he was sitting beside me in his floating chair, the next minute he was gone like the wind. Well, actually, gone *with* the wind. Yep, he took the Zephyr Express back to Key West. At least that's what *I* think.

Naturally, a dozen WWOWzers immediately took chase. Our strongest swimmer, Charlene, actually got within a few yards of him before she was called back because she was dangerously too far away. Susie's captain told us her yacht drew too much water for those shallows that Mr. Stud was sailing right over, so we would not be able to rescue Charlene if she got into trouble. We had not brought a kayak along, either. Of course, if Charlene had caught Mr. Stud and then got a cramp, I am sure he would rescue her *if* he noticed her.

So Charlene gave up and reluctantly swam back to the yacht. All of us girls felt pretty bad about losing our beloved mascot, Mr. Stud.

Judy sobbing on Mr. Stud's shorts.

All we had left to remember him by was his shorts. So they wouldn't get wet, Susanna had taken them off him before he had gone into the water. He was always a very modest skinny-dipper because his birthday suit was a pair of blue skintight swimming briefs tighter than Superman's.

The scent of a man—as intoxicating as that new car smell.

If he knew he was going to spend the day float-ing on the water, his choice for personal grooming was Aqua Valve.

We toasted Mr. Stud's time with us, the Wild Women on the Water, with many glasses of champagne.

We speculated about his fate. Would some toothy critter like a shark or barracuda get him? Would he get crabs? Was he trying to reach a par-amour in a rubber goods store on Duval Street—a "buysexual"—or maybe another vinyl blow-up doll like himself, but of the opposite sex, perhaps a Suzy the Floozy? Would he reach his destination? Or would his deflated, lifeless body be found on Earth Day, some twenty years from now, on the bottom of the bay by scuba divers volunteering for ocean cleanup? I pictured his face hairy with hydroids. In two or three days, would somebody see Mr. Stud floating face down in the Gulf of Mexico, mistake him for a dead body, and call the Coast Guard? What if some frail old lady beachcomber comes upon him wedged between the rocks and has a heart attack? Being women, we felt guilty. We felt bad.

We poured another round of drinks and raised our glasses in salute to our favorite mascot, Mr. Stud, and wished him Godspeed. We felt better. I said a silent prayer that he would pass safely by the Channel Five Bridge and that awful turtle.

Wild Women fighting over Mr. Stud.

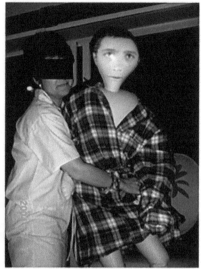

Getting kisses all over his body inflates Mr. Stud's ego!

Mr. Stud's $1/kiss WWOW fundraiser.

Being kissed by Wild Women on the
Water curls Mr. Stud's toes!

Yay! We made it!

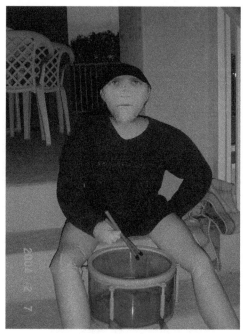

Mr. Stud the Beatnik drums to a different beat.

Mr. Stud is full of hot air, but if he blows in Linda's
ear, she'll follow him anywhere! They both will be
sorely missed. The doll will be difficult to replace.
Our friend Linda is impossible to replace.

**You never know when a manatee will
join you while you're swimming.**

Masked bandit in palm tree hideout.

Ibises roosting or nesting on a mangrove key.

Cuban-Style Pork Fish
By Gail Feddern

Pork fish, trigger fish, or ocean tally fillets
1 bell pepper
1 large onion
1 large potato
Mojo Criollo
1 slice of bacon
1 Tbs. olive oil
salt, black pepper, thyme, and sage to taste

Cut fish and vegetables into bite-size pieces. Marinate fish in Mojo Criollo sauce in refrigerator while preparing rest of ingredients. Heat oil in pan and add potatoes; when lightly browned but not cooked, add rest of ingredients and cook until done. Serve alone or with cooked rice.

Note: This meal can be wrapped in a foil package and cooked on the barbeque grill.

Northwoods Salmon
By Suzy Burrows

brown mustard
salmon steaks or fillets
butter
maple syrup
1 tsp. brown sugar, 1/8 tsp. ginger, or 1/8 tsp.
 cinnamon (optional)

Slather brown mustard on salmon pieces. Let set for 5 minutes. Caramelize butter (and one of the optional ingredients, if desired) in a pan, and stir in maple syrup. Place salmon in pan and cook one side, then the other.

Grouper Parmesan

2 lb. grouper fillets
1 C. sour cream
1/4 C. grated Parmesan cheese
1 Tbs. lemon juice
1 Tbs. grated onion
1/2 tsp. salt
dash of hot pepper sauce
paprika
chopped parsley
pam, butter, or cooking oil

Skin fillets and cut into serving size portions. Place in single layer in a well-greased baking dish 12×8×2 inches. Combine remaining ingredients except paprika and parsley. Spread sour cream mix over fish. Sprinkle with paprika. Bake at 350 degrees for 25–30 minutes or till flaky. Garnish with parsley. Serves 6.

A Boating Safety/Rescue Tip: In fog, or if your boat broke down and you don't have a working radar or radar reflector, you can *improvise a radar reflector by stringing together aluminum cans or aluminum foil pans and hanging them from the highest point on your boat.*

Idle Hands

Keys people are a little weird, with a quirky sense of humor. What makes us that way? My friends and I have often debated the subject. Is it algae on the brain, perhaps from inhaling too deeply the intoxicating ocean breezes, or maybe deposited there by sludge and questionable residues from our only drinking water source, the Aqueduct Authority's pipeline? Of course, a lot of our residents don't believe in drinking water; in their case it might be due to Keys disease (there are probably more AA meetings in the Keys per capita than anyplace else). Or perhaps it's simply due to our broiling hot sun beating down on inadequately protected pates. The Florida Keys are latitude 25, which is located in the subtropics, after all. Wearing a visor may help protect your eyes, but it does nothing at all for your head.

However, I like to think Keys people are kooky because living in paradise means no stress, but there is a narrow line between relaxation and boredom. They've learned to walk that fine line by having *fun!*

If you go west through Tavernier Creek, turn left, and go south a little ways, you will find a perfect example of this silliness—known by the Locals as Toilet Seat Creek or Toilet Seat Pass. Let's hope NOAA leaves it alone.

Overview of Toilet Seat Pass.

WWOW boat passing.

Another crappy day in paradise.

Circe and Steve.

Crap trap.

To hell with mass—here's where
we'll shit our winter ass.

Too bad your half-assed relatives
found your spot in the Keys.

SpongeBob.

Eileen L-F holds spruced up WWOW toilet
seat with wine cork embellishment.

Mounting the WWOW toilet seat.

The refurbished WWOW toilet seat fully
installed at Toilet Seat Pass.

SURVIVAL NUTRITIONAL NEEDS

Ancient mariners would stave off scurvy somewhat by eating fermented products, such as sauerkraut. Organ meats, brains, and fresh raw meat and fish are the most nutritious, and ships carried live animals for food. As long as the crew could chew on rare steaks and such, they remained healthy. Scurvy wouldn't appear until they ran out of fresh meat, fruit, and vegetables and had to dig into the hardtack biscuits and other preserved stores with long shelf lives.

British people got the nickname limeys because their sailing ships carried limes to combat scurvy. Before that ships the world over had the problem of their crews weakening and dying from the dreaded disease. All their captains knew was that they needed to feed the seamen fresh meat and vegetables or they'd get scurvy. Corned beef and salt cod were not sufficient to ward off scurvy because dried foods don't contain enough Vitamin C, which is the nutrient the body needs or it will succumb to scurvy. Heat deteriorates Vitamin C.

It's a pity no one realized that all they had to do was scoop up some seaweed and eat it. In addition to all sorts of vitamins and minerals, seaweeds worldwide have iodine, which aids in flushing radiation poisoning from the body, as well as being an antiseptic for wounds.

Note: *dragging your sea anchor can capture plankton, which is rich in Vitamin C and other essential nutrients.*

Of course, Vitamin C is not the only nutritional requirement for us mammals. We need calories in the form of carbohydrates, proteins, and fats. We also need vitamins, minerals, and enzymes. Among some of the more important ones are Vitamin A, thiamine, riboflavin, niacin, calcium, phosphorus, and iron. And we need fiber to move it all along our digestive system. **Note:** *you can make calcium in the wild by grinding into a fine powder coral rock, seashells, limestone, egg shells, or boiled-soft or roasted bones.*

Sugars and starches are carbohydrates. Commercial sugar is made from sugarcane in the south and large sugar beets (mangle) in the North. Honey and fruits are natural sources for the sugar fructose. Starches come from grains, legumes (dried beans, peas, and lentils), and potatoes. It is recommended that you eat around 300 grams of carbo-hydrates a day, or roughly 50 percent of your diet should be carbohydrates.

Women should not go below a 1,200- or 1,500-calorie diet, even when wanting to lose weight. Men require twice as many calories. Soldier's rations are around 3,000 to 4,500 calories per day.

To refresh your own recollection of basic nutrition: Our bodies run on calories for energy and maintenance. One calorie is a unit of energy. Calories fuel our bodies from three sources: carbo-hydrates, protein, and fat. Roughly half of your daily calorie intake should be from carbohydrates (45–65 percent), around 30 percent from fats, and the rest, around 10-35 percent, from protein. Protein builds and maintains our muscles. Carbohydrates give us energy. Fats are necessary to utilize certain vitamins. Fat insulates and cushions our body. Whatever their source, unused calories stick to our bodies as fat (tell me about it!) to be stored and used later, if needed. At 120 calories per tablespoon., fat has the highest concentration of calories.

But you don't absolutely have to have carbo-hydrates like you do have to have fat and protein for your body to stay alive. Have you ever heard of rabbit starvation? You can actually starve to death while eating wild rabbits because they are so lean that they do not have enough fat to sustain you. (You can avoid that by eating the internal organs, such as liver, kidneys, heart, brains, and stomach contents [made more palatable in soup], as well as eyeballs and skin.) In spite of that, protein is probably the most essential nutrient because it is the only one that will sustain muscle. Contrary to popular belief, fat does not turn to muscle. Nor will carbohydrate make muscle. Yet protein can do carbohydrate's job and supply energy when called upon. Too much protein, too much carbohydrate, and too much fat will be stored on your body as fat for an energy source of calories to be used when you exercise. Bottom line is, in a survival situation, you must seek out sources of protein and fat; usually that means meat from wild animals of any kind, fish or shellfish, birds and eggs, fat from them or oil from plant sources, such as coconuts and avocados. Of course, you can find both protein and fat in just one little critter, and they're plentiful here in Florida—palmetto bugs, anyone? I'm sorry, but I would have to be desperately hungry, and they would have to be roasted crispy before I'd ever consider crunching down on roaches or bugs of any kind, Les Stroud* and Bear Grylls** notwithstanding!

Note: A useful website on the subject of survival nutrition is http://www.simplesurvival.net/nutrition.htm.

---

*   of TV show, *Survivorman*
** of TV show, *Man vs. Wild*

Hog Snapper Teriyaki
By Gail Feddern

fillets of hog snapper or other fish
sliced Swiss cheese or processed Swiss cheese
sliced mushrooms, fresh (preferred) or canned
Kikkoman's teriyaki sauce
Pam cooking spray
cooked white rice

Place fish fillets in a shallow baking dish sprayed with Pam. Pour 1 Tbs. of teriyaki sauce over each fillet, plus 1 Tbs. for the dish. Cover with mushrooms and place 1 slice of cheese on each fillet. Cover dish and bake at 400 degrees for 35 or 40 minutes if using frozen fillets or until done. Serve over cooked white rice.

Baked Fish
By Gail Feddern

fish fillets

lemon or lime juice

bread crumbs (I use Italian-style)

bran, 1 rounded tsp. / fillet, sprinkled on or blended with bread crumbs (optional)

chopped scallions

chopped fresh tomatoes

1 Tbs. grated Parmesan cheese

dots of diet margarine or buttery spray

Assemble ingredients in above order in a baking pan and bake at 325 degrees for 15 minutes.

Note: This is a great-tasting low-calorie recipe.

Gail's Broiled Cod Fish Fillets

2 frozen or fresh cod fish fillets
1/2 C. sour cream, mixed with 1 dollop of tomato
   soup concentrate
lemon butter sauce
dashes of paprika and black pepper

Spoon lemon butter sauce on fillets. Sprinkle with paprika and pepper. Broil fillets 6–8 minutes on one side. Turn and spoon lemon butter sauce on other side. Broil for 6 minutes. Slather with sour cream mix and cook 2 more minutes or until flaky.

Sautéed Fish Fillets
By Gail Feddern

fish fillets
butter/olive oil
medium yellow onion
paprika
onion powder
garlic powder
salt
pepper

Slice the onion and brown it in a pan with olive oil. Season fillets with paprika, onion powder, garlic powder, salt, and pepper. Remove the onions. Melt butter in pan. Put fillets in pan and sauté. When one side is done, flip over and cover with onions. Cook until done. Note: I usually make this dish with hog snapper, but it also works well with lesser fish, such as trigger fish, porgy, and grunts.

Cooking Tip: When **pan-frying fish**, you don't want to use a heavy batter. Instead of using flour, cornmeal, cereal, or bread crumbs, try dusting your fillets with rice flour, which is naturally gluten-free. It gives it a light, delicate touch, yet it's nicely crispy. Fry with a garlic bud in olive oil.

Another breading material, for **either fried or broiled fish,** is Snyder's of Hanover honey mustard and onion pretzel pieces, ground fine with a rolling pin or liquor/wine bottle. Its delicious flavor is unique.

Moon's Margarita
(Stolen from Joe's Bar)

4 oz. Triple Sec
4 oz. Key lime juice
8 oz. to kill ya (tequila)
5 heapin' tsp. sugar or 5 pkg. of Sweet 'n Low
(mostly to your taste)

Combine all ingredients and serve over ice in a glass or put in a blender with ice and blend.

Options:
Top with Grand Marnier or less costly Cointreau.
May add little Curacao for blue color.

Salt the rim of glass if desired and serve with a slice of lime on glass.
Drink responsibly.

DON'T TAMPER WITH TAPIRS!

(A true adventure)
By Gloria Crum

My fellow Wild Woman Jane Martin and I have traveled to many interesting, different places in the world. Several years ago, we were in Ecuador, having just returned from a Galapagos Island sailboat trip, where we visited most of the islands. By the way, Ecuador means "equator," and that's where it is.

We were spending a week of free time in Quito, Ecuador, before taking off on our next adventure—a week at Sacha Lodge on the Amazon River.

While in Quito, we hired a driver and car for one day. The driver, a local Ecuadorian, drove us to Pasochoa National Park in the Andes Mountains. It was Sunday and a holiday. All the guides were off celebrating. We were assured by our driver and the lady accepting the admission charge that it was perfectly safe for us to hike in the park unguided as all the trails were clearly marked in various colors.

We decided to hike the yellow trail, and off we went, just we two. It was just a narrow path;

one side went downhill, the other uphill. After approximately one hour of enjoyable sight-seeing, we noticed a rather large animal lying in the path ahead. It was the size of a large boar. There was no alternative route, so we shouted, hoping to scare it away. In the meantime, I was trying to get a picture of the animal. Jane was climbing onto a large rock. Instead of running away, the enraged animal, a mountain tapir, came running madly toward me and attacked with all its might—goring holes into my right leg, about four inches above the ankle. I was frightened as the animal was raging mad, ready to kill, but I made a fist and, with all my might, smashed the animal in its snout! It started shrieking and turned a bit. I then punched it in the side stomach area, and as it turned to run, I hit it again in its rear end. It ran off.

Luckily, only two places on my leg were deep wounds, the others scratches, not bleeding profusely. We took a shortcut and one hour later returned to our point of beginning where our driver and car were waiting. Fortunately, our driver had a doctor friend in the nearby town. The doctor came to his office from home on a Sunday afternoon. He cleansed the wound, gave me an antibiotic shot, several medications to treat the wound in the future, pain killers, etc., and only charged fifteen US dollars. He hesitatingly took the twenty I gave him.

I kept treating the wound on the next part of our trip to the Jungle Lodge. All was healing well.

When we returned home, I contacted the US government and state health departments, and I was advised to take the shots for rabies (ouch!). They hurt, but all was OK.

Drunken Shrimp
By Christine Clarke

1 doz. big, fresh shrimps
1 jar Emmeril's vodka sauce
fresh peas
ziti
garlic
olive oil
onion

Sauté oil, garlic, onion, and shrimp. Boil water, cook, and drain pasta. Heat vodka sauce. Add peas, shrimp mixture, and pasta.

Serve with a green salad.

Irma's Clam Soup
By Irma Woodward

This can be a Crock-Pot recipe.

one 51 oz. can of clams (available at warehouse
    stores, e.g., Sam's, Costco, BJ's)
1 stick of butter
dash of pepper
3–4 stalks celery, chopped fine
1 large onion, chopped fine
1 pt. heavy whipping cream

Sauté celery and onion in a stick of butter. (No
substitutes!)

Add clams with juice and cream. Put in a dash
of pepper. Heat, but do *not* boil!

Very tasty—thinner than chowder because there
are *no* potatoes. Low-carb friendly!

**Canoeing and kayaking are favorite pastimes
with Wild Women on the Water.**

We do it in the spring or summer in the Upper Keys at places like Indian Key or Dove Creek. In October or November, we paddle a river farther up the state that our scouts have selected for us in advance. We've canoed on the Manatee River, the Peace River, the Fish-Eating Creek, and the Loxahatchee River. We make it a weekend event. Friday night we find a local watering hole where we eat, party, and dance. The rest of the weekend we spend camping and paddling. If it's around Halloween, we usually dress up in costumes and do fun activities Saturday night. Sunday morning, after a WWOW breakfast, we pack up and head home.

Kayak Safety Tip: To make yourself more visible, especially at night, *wrap reflective tape on your paddle* (near the base of the blade). As you paddle, the motion of reflected light from sun, lights, or moonlight draws attention so other boats can steer clear. Wave the paddle in the air if you need help. (This tip is from http://kayaking.fateback.com.)

Mr. Hand gets fresh with Rebekah; he just can't keep his hand off those Wild Women ghouls!

Wendy's Grandma's Famous Chocolate Cake with Chocolate Icing

By Wendy Russell Diaz

2 C. sifted flour

2 C. sugar

1/2 C. buttermilk

2 eggs

1 Tbs. cinnamon

1 Tbs. vanilla (or rum, as Wendy likes it)

1 tsp. baking soda

1 stick butter

1/2 C. Crisco

1 C. water (or 1/2 C. water and 1/2 C. rum, as Wendy likes it)

4 Tbs. cocoa

Grease and flour a 13×9 inch baking pan.

In a large bowl, mix the flour and sugar, and set aside.

In a smaller bowl, mix buttermilk, eggs, cinnamon, vanilla or rum, and baking soda.

In saucepan, mix butter, Crisco, water (or water and rum), and cocoa. Bring this to a boil and pour over the flour and sugar mixture. Then pour in the buttermilk mixture.

Mix it all very well, and then pour into the baking pan. Bake at 350 degrees for 25 to 30 minutes.

Chocolate Icing
for Chocolate Cake

4 Tbs. cocoa
6 Tbs. milk
1 Tbs. vanilla
1 stick butter
1 box powdered sugar

Put all ingredients except sugar in a saucepan and bring to a boil. Add the box of powdered sugar. Remove from heat. Beat very well with mixer and immediately pour over chocolate cake.

Brisket a' la Claire
By Claire Lang

1 whole brisket of beef
1 pkg. Lipton onion soup, dry
6 stalks celery, cut up
2 C. mushrooms, cut into halves
4 carrots, cut up
3 C. red wine
3 C. water, as needed
1 Tbs. garlic bits in oil
sprinkle of Lawry's seasoned salt
1/2 C. catsup (optional)
1 medium onion, cut up (optional)

On high heat, brown brisket on both sides in a large roasting pan.

Put rest of ingredients on top, cover, and cook inside oven at 325 degrees for 4 hours; check occasionally to see if more liquid needs to be added to prevent drying out or burning, and add water as necessary.

Seafood Soup
By Jane Martin

1 clove garlic
1 small onion
2 Tbs. olive oil
1 can diced tomatoes
1 can tomato soup
2 C. seafood (crab, shrimp, lobster), cooked
1 C. half and half cream
splash of sherry (optional)

Dice garlic and onion and sauté in olive oil. Add tomatoes, tomato soup, and seafood. Heat, then add cream. Serve alone or over rice.

(A little sherry is great!)

Fish Bourguignon
by Jeanine Stelzner

2 lb. flaked (chopped raw) white fish
1 medium onion, finely chopped
1/2 lb. sliced Portobello mushroom
2 cloves garlic, minced
salt and pepper to taste
1–2 Tbs. Italian seasoning
olive oil or butter for frying
8 oz. fish/chicken stock
4 oz. white wine
4 oz. grated cheese
6 oz. sour cream
1 Tbs. ready-made mustard (Tasty is best)

Decoration
Hot cooked asparagus spears

Fry onion and garlic in oil until softened. Add herbs and seasoning, mushroom, liquids, and fish, and cook gently until fish is cooked. Adjust seasoning. Reduce liquid over low heat. Stir in sour cream, mustard, and grated cheese just before serving. Stir until blended.

Serve with asparagus, crusty, warm bread, and mashed potatoes.

Shrimp and Mushroom Soup
By Cynthia McGregor (Boerner)

1 can cream of mushroom soup
1 can cream of potato soup
1 qt. half and half
1/2 gal. milk
1/2 C. white wine
3/4 tsp. curry powder
1 tsp. dry chives
1 Tbs. salt
1 Tbs. white pepper
1/2 bunch scallions
2 lb. raw shrimp, cut up bite-size
1 can mushrooms, sliced thin

Drain mushrooms. Peel and cut up shrimp. Cut up scallions. Place all ingredients in large pot and simmer at low heat for 4 hours to blend flavor.

**Sharon throws a cast net to catch bait fish
to use in trolling for dolphin, etc.**

Things I learned from fishing with WWOW members are: Have several ballyhoos rigged ready to go. Leave the first dolphin in the water until you catch the next. Have cooler positioned and lid open so you can swing the fish directly into it if the action is hot! If blood *does* get on the boat, clean it up now before it dries. Follow the birds. Troll thirty feet away from weeds.

Sally and Sharon, two of WWOW's best fishing champs

Every year, WWOW schedules a fishing tournament amongst the girls. They are free to fish wherever they like: backcountry (bayside), oceanside, in-shore, off a dock or bridge, on patch reefs in Hawk Channel, on the reef, or offshore in the Gulf Stream. They may fish however they like: hook-and-line fishing, bottom fishing, drift fishing, or trolling. Sharon and Sally caught these dolphins (mahi-mahi) while trolling eight or ten miles out in the dark blue waters of the gulf stream. The rules are earliest lines in the water at 8:00 a.m., latest lines out of the water by 2:00 p.m.

Later, after cleaning fish (if they didn't catch and release) and getting themselves cleaned up and changing clothes, everybody meets at a designated member's home for bragging or whining, and wining. Food and refreshments are served. Awards and prizes are presented for biggest fish, most fish, most unusual fish, and best hard luck story.

Mango/Mango or Mango/Mangrove Snapper

mangrove snapper
diced tomato
diced mango
blanched onions
butter
tin or aluminum foil
salt
cilantro

Blanch onions first. In the foil, place the fish, tomato, blanched onions, and butter. Fold up the foil. Bake in oven at 350 degrees for more or less 10 minutes. Add salt and cilantro after baking.

This is **Sue Sigel's** favorite recipe *that her husband, Bill, cooks for her!*

Susie's Bleu Cheese Fish
By Susie Temkin

Any fish (yellowtail is excellent)
1/2 tub bleu cheese
3 Tbs. light butter

Mix the bleu cheese with the light butter and melt together in the microwave oven. Pour over the fish and broil till done.

Note: *Make up extra sauce to pour over the fish after it comes out of the oven, and to serve at the table.*

Cooking Tip from Susie: She uses the book *365 Ways to Cook Chicken* to cook fish!

Susie's Broiled Fish Recipe
By Susie Temkin

fillets of fish
breadcrumbs
scallions
tomatoes
cheese

Take fillets of fish and cover with breadcrumbs and scallions; put under broiler till almost done. Dice tomatoes and cheese and mix them together; pour over fish and brown to finish.

The Uni-Knot

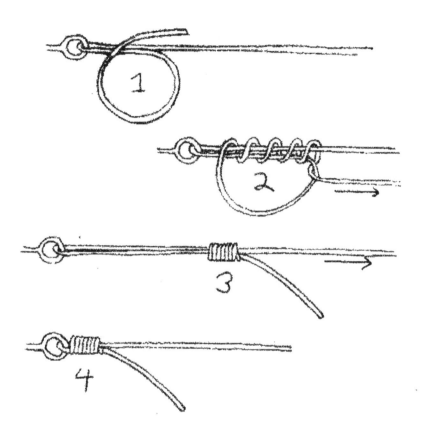

If you feel you want to learn only one knot to go fishing, the uni-knot is for you! It is versatile, strong, simple, and easy to use. The directions are self-explanatory if you follow the illustration above.

Tackle Tip: When tying tackle with nylon monofilament line, *always* moisten it with water or saliva before you tighten the knot. For years, my terminal tackle terminated, just when a fish was on it! It wasn't until I took a "Ladies, Let's Go Fishing!" seminar that I learned the secret is to snug it up tight by wetting it first. Then I stopped losing my fishing rigs.

How to Handle Your Catch

Part of this book is a cookbook, so I assume you are going to fillet and release, not catch and release. (If you were going to catch and release, you would wet your hands or a cloth and gently set the fish in the water; if he's exhausted, gently move him through the water as if he were swimming, to aerate his gills.)

Experts recommend that you gut the fish, spread open the cavity and place it on ice in your ice chest with the drain open so that body fluids won't pool and make it taste bad. Busy fishermen close the drain and throw the fish whole into an ice chest with ice, and add some seawater to super-chill the catch. Did you know that a grouper can live for up to two hours out of water? If you can't ice him down, stash him in the shade and cover him with a wet cloth or burlap sack.

Lobsters should be kept alive in a mesh bag or burlap sack and dipped several times in the ocean every hour or so until you get them home. Keep them out of the sun.

Fish can be butterflied (best for pan-frying small fish like grunts, or for smoking) or cut into fillets or steaks. Leave the skin on if you plan to smoke it.

Important! *Please* **don't ever scale a fish while he's still alive.**

Yes, *fish* do *feel pain!* In fact, any living creature that has nerves will feel pain if you hurt it. So please be a kind person and humanely kill the animal first. After all, how would *you* like to be skinned alive?

Freezing is the most popular method of preserving a surplus catch. Locals like to freeze seafood in salted water. They claim it extends the quality up to a year. Thoroughly cleaned waxed cardboard milk cartons are ideal for this. That's great if you usually have a big gang to cook for, but I have a small family, so I prefer to put serving size portions in fold-lock sandwich bags, and then stuff them all into a Ziploc freezer bag.

Also, you can buy a vacuum sealer. You put the food in these special plastic bags and use the vacuum sealer to suck the air out, causing the bag to cling to the surface of the food, thereby reducing freezer burn.

Whatever method you use, be sure to label the outside of the container with the date. I mark mine with a permanent marker. Eat up the seafood within five or six months. After that length of time, it can start to taste fishy. If it's close, or a little past its expiration date, hold it under cold running water and rub it. That will remove the bacteria on the surface.

If it's *way* out of date, no need to throw it away— just relabel it and use it for bait or chum. (For those of you who are not yet saltwater fishermen, chum is ground up fish scraps used as a fish attractant. It can be scooped up and thrown at a school of fish or placed in a mesh bag and hung over the side of the boat to let the current lure the fish with tantalizing smells and hors d'oeuvres of ew-de-phew. An occasional shake of the bag re-excites the fish.)

Fisherman's Tip Regarding Eating Snook: *Remove the skin before cooking, because it makes the fish taste soapy!* People always rave about how delicious snook is, but they never tell you to skin it. I finally caught one, and because I didn't know any better, I cut it into steaks and cooked it without skinning it first. I had to throw it out. I blamed my dishwasher for not rinsing the pan I cooked it in!

How to Release a Gut-Hooked Fish, Unharmed

There will come a time when you want to or need to let a fish go. You want him to live, perhaps to catch another day. Fishing and marine ecology depend on healthy fish stocks, and we all have an obligation to sustain the supply if we wish to keep on fishing, not just because the government considers fishing a privilege, not a right.

Authorities recommend using circle hooks because they work well on most species, usually hooking in the side of the mouth. Remember not to set the hook when fishing with a circle hook, or it will come right out of the fish's mouth. But don't give him enough time to swallow it either because circle hooks are more difficult to remove from the gut. To catch the fish, just pull steadily.

Hard baits are less likely to be swallowed whole by fish. If you only want to catch and release, then before going fishing, you should bend down the barbs that are attached to the points of your hooks, both regular and treble.

Fishing is fun for us, but it's a life-or-death struggle for the fish, and a certain percentage die, even when they get away. Many slowly starve to death. Yes, fish hooks eventually rust away, especially in saltwater, but probably not in time to save the fish. Avoid using stainless steel hooks for that reason. Tinned hooks and bronze hooks are much better choices because they decay far more quickly. Personally, I use thin wire bronze (freshwater) J-hooks when fishing in my canal for snapper. The tannin in the water makes them practically invisible, and when they get snagged on rocks, I don't lose my rig; they straighten out, I reel them in, and I bend them back into shape with pliers. It saves me a lot of aggravation.

You should always carry a hook remover in your tackle box. Two types are commonly used in the Keys. One is a long metal lever-type pinchers, which is especially good with toothy critters. The other is a red plastic "dog bone" stick. With the latter, choose which knob is the more suitable size. Take the slack out of the fishing line and insert the line into a slot on the knob, push the knob into the gullet and, with the line still taut, push the stick toward the tail, engaging the shank of the hook and lifting it up and out.

If you don't have a hook disgorger, look around to improvise. Do you have a bait rigging needle? The principle behind the dog bone disgorger is to cover the barb so you can lift the hook out without causing damage to the fish. So see if you can substitute the rigging needle; slip the open eye of the needle over the line, push on the hook, and lift it out. You might have to open the needle's eye more to allow it to slip over the hook's eye first. Barring that, maybe you have another, larger hook with an open eye large enough to slip over the hook's eye and engage the shank of the hook. Or perhaps you can fashion a dehooker out of a stiff piece of wire, like a coat hanger.

If you have no hook remover, you can use your fingers or long-nose pliers or perhaps forceps. First, put on gloves, if you have them, to protect against the fish's teeth, if he has them. Cut the line, leaving an eighteen-inch leader. With one hand, hold the lower jaw so the mouth opens wide. With the other hand, gently pull the line to expose the hook eye and shank as much as possible without hurting the fish. Put the taut line under your thumb that's holding the inside of the jaw to hold the hook in place until you perform the next step. With long-nose pliers or your fingers, reach through the gill opening closest to the fish's body (you can go through the first or last gill opening, but never between the other gills), grip the hook eye, and rotate the hook horizontally so that the eye points toward the tail. This horizontal hook movement rotates the barb sideways and frees it from the fish. Then reach in through the mouth and grip the curve of the hook and lift it out. Go to YouTube and search the site for hook removal for illustrations of this procedure.

If the hook still won't come out, don't cut the line off. Release the fish with the eighteen-inch length of line *minus sinker*, etc., to better allow him to eat, experts say.

Fisherman's Tips: When taking pictures of large fish, support their bodies horizontally rather than holding them by the jaw. And *never* hold them by the gills. When removing a hook from a fish's jaw, leave the fish in the water, if possible. If it's going to take a while, gently lay the fish down on a wet towel. If you need to bring a fish into the boat, use a landing net if you can; scoop it headfirst because if you touch its tail it will explode out of the net in a burst of renewed energy! If you have to use a gaff, gaff the jaw to minimize damage to the fish. Never gaff eyes, gills, or underside.

The Best Way to Remove a Hook from Skin

Accidents happen, so sometimes people get hooked by mistake. The best way to take the hook out is to use the press-and-snatch string method. It's the *least* painful and damaging method of removal. However, if someone is hooked in the face or some other crucial place, the leader should be removed and the person taken to a doctor or emergency ward. Otherwise, this method works fine for torso and extremities—firm flesh, but nothing floppy like earlobes, lips, etc.

Before you begin, have everyone stand back out of the way because the hook will fly out, and you don't want it to impale anyone else.

You might want to numb the area first with a piece of ice or Benadryl spray, mostly to allay your patient's fears. The actual pain is slight and quickly over with. Take a stout piece of string, cord, ribbon, or heavy-duty fishing line, about a yard long, and double it around the curve of the hook. Simultaneously, press down on the eye of the hook and toward the curve of the hook and at the same time give a strong, quick yank on the string. It should come right out. Follow the illustration below.

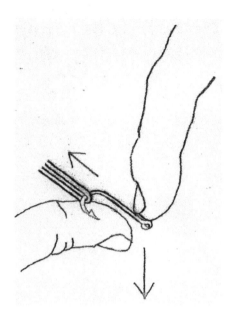

As with all puncture wounds, encourage it to bleed, wash with soap and water, and apply antiseptic and a Band-Aid.

Beverly's Seven-Layer Salad
By Beverly Hooper

A large, glass bowl (so you can see the layers)

Dressing
1½ C. mayonnaise
2 Tbs. sugar
2/3 C. Parmesan cheese, grated

Salad
Lettuce, chopped and shredded
1 red onion, sliced
10 oz. frozen peas, thawed
8 to 10 oz. pkg. shredded cheddar cheese
4 hard-boiled eggs, sliced or crumbled
1 lb. bacon, cooked and crumbled

Start building your seven-layer salad: for the bottom layer, line the bowl with one inch of lettuce. Add some red onion, some peas, some cheddar cheese, and a layer of hard-boiled egg. Repeat each successive layer until you have seven layers. Use the dressing above. Sprinkle the top with bacon crumbles.

Famous Smoked Fish Dip
By Daryl Stone

1 lb. smoked fish (kingfish, tuna, or a great time
    to use barracuda!)
1/2 medium sweet onion, chopped
1/4 C. olive pieces with pimento
olive oil
mayonnaise
olive juice

Grind smoked fish in food processor. Add onion
and olive pieces.

Add olive oil, olive juice, and mayonnaise to
bind.

Serve with crackers. It serves a group of people.

Helpful Hint: **Take a piece of *duct tape, adhesive tape, masking or painter's tape, or other sticky tape* and tape a spare car key to the back of your cell phone.** It's not really a good idea to keep a spare key hidden in a magnetic box under your car, because most car thieves know about that little trick, and if it's a particularly desirable car and a particularly determined car thief, well…

Another use for sticky tape: Use it to remove fine bristles on cactus pears or any difficult to see irritants stuck in your skin, such as bristle-worm hairs or fire sponge spicules.

Seared Tuna
By Daryl Stone

fresh tuna steak, not frozen!
extra-virgin olive oil
toasted sesame seed oil
Everglades seasoning
Crab Man seasoning (use Old Bay sparingly if
    Crab Man is unavailable)
black sesame seeds
condiments: wasabi, pickled ginger and soy
    sauce

Cut tuna into thick steaks, pat dry with paper towels. Wet both sides with extra-virgin olive oil and toasted sesame seed oil. Sprinkle both sides with Everglades or Crab Man seasoning. Coat very heavily with black sesame seeds. Fill frying plan with 1/4 inch extra-virgin olive oil. Add 3 Tbs. toasted sesame seed oil. Heat oil to a temperature of approximately 500 degrees. Flash sear both sides of tuna approximately 30 seconds on each side. (The middle of the fish should be red.) Serve with wasabi, pickled ginger, and soy sauce.

Cooking Tips from Judy O'Hara Vetrick:

1. Top your fish fillets or steaks with mayonnaise before putting on the grill or baking in the oven. This really gives them a great taste and keeps them moist.

2. For larger fish, like dolphin, wahoo, or kingfish for instance, try baking in the oven with white wine, salt, pepper, and your favorite herbs (an Italian combo is good). This really wakes up the taste buds and complements the natural goodness of the fresh fish.

Simply Yummy Appetizer
By Marie Henson

1 lb. deveined, cleaned shrimp (20–25 count is
    good)
jalapeno peppers
1/2 lb. bacon cut in half
butter, melted
Everglades seasoning

Blot shrimp dry with paper towels. Split and remove the seeds from about eight of the jalapeno peppers and cut into slices about 1/3 the length of the shrimp. Wrap a slice of bacon around each shrimp and slice of pepper. Baste with melted butter seasoned with 1/8 tsp. Everglades seasoning. Grill till shrimp is pink, usually about 2–3 minutes per side. *Don't overcook or the shrimp will get tough!*

LIFE-SAVING TIPS
REGARDING A STROKE

If you suspect someone *might* be having a stroke, do this test:

1. Ask them to *smile*.
2. Ask them to *raise both arms*.
3. Ask them to *speak a simple sentence* (coherently); an example would be "It's a nice day today."

If they can't do *all* of these simple things, then get them to an emergency ward *immediately*! Either dial 911 and call for an ambulance or drive them yourself, after calling first to alert the hospital so that medical personnel can be ready to take them immediately. *Time is crucial!* Death or permanent disability can often be avoided if the patient is administered antistroke medication within the first forty-five or sixty minutes.

A friend of mine's daughter came home with all the physical symptoms of a stroke, e.g., no control over her arms and legs, *except* she was coherent. It depends on whereabouts in the brain the stroke is. In her case it was not in the cognitive part of her brain, so she could think clearly and speak pretty well. Her mother rushed her to the hospital. They kept asking her if she had taken some substance that she wasn't supposed to and which one it was. Even though she vehemently denied taking any illegal drugs at all, they did not believe her because she was a young person, only nineteen years old. It is unusual for someone so young to get a stroke, but it has happened, even to very young children. It is not unusual for young people these days to do illegal recreational drugs, but that was not the case with this girl. This girl was plagued with migraine headaches, so she was on daily hormone therapy to prevent them. Also, she smoked. *Those were three factors that put her at risk for a stroke.* Regrettably, *the hospital sent her home without medicating her at all!* Fortunately, another hospital gave her the treatment she needed and she eventually recovered.

A stroke is a "brain attack." It occurs when oxygen can't nourish the brain cells. Most strokes are caused by a blood clot blocking an artery. (This type of stroke is called thrombo-embolic, and 70 percent of the strokes that affect middle aged and older women are this kind.) The other type of stroke is the bleeding kind (called hemorrhagic), which occurs when a blood vessel in or to the brain suddenly bursts. High blood pressure and aneurysms can cause these strokes.

Antistroke medications may still be beneficial if they are given within three hours. Not so, studies have shown, if the time lapse is six hours or more. Bear in mind that hospitals are usually busiest on nights and weekends. However, hospitals do triage, meaning they put the most serious cases at the head of the line. A supervisor at the emergency ward of Mariners' Hospital in Tavernier, Florida, reassured me that strokes, heart attacks, and asthma patients get priority, followed by flu patients (at least in the fall of 2005). Know ahead of time what you want to do if you or a loved one gets a stroke, and discuss it with those close to you.

To formulate your emergency stroke plan, call the hospitals closest to you, now, and ask them these questions:

- How long before a stroke patient gets treated? (Mariners said within minutes to under an hour, which is excellent!)

- Do they get a CT scan right away, or do they have to wait for a specialist? (Mariners said they don't wait; they give the patient a CT scan right away.)
- Is the specialist—a neurologist—always at the hospital, or does he have to come from his home? (At Mariners it varies, depending on his shift. They have at least two neurologists on staff.)
- If he's at home, how soon can he get to the hospital? (The Mariners supervisor I talked to didn't know.)
- Does the hospital stock tPA (tissue plasminogen activator, a drug used to treat possible strokes due to blockage)? Time is critical if they have to send out for it, and it used to be that only a few hospitals kept it on hand. (Mariners, I'm happy to report, says they have it there.)
- Does the hospital have corticosteroids and IV medications to prevent brain swelling? (Most hospitals, including Mariners, do.)
- Does the hospital carry medications to help protect the brain from damage and lack of oxygen? (Mariners has some.)

What do you do if you are at sea on a private boat when someone has a stroke and it will take too many hours before they can get medical help? Use your marine radiotelephone or cell phone (if it's within range) to call for help. The Coast Guard and many hospitals (including Mariners) have medevac helicopters. While you are on the line, ask the medical people if there is anything you can do while you are waiting for them to come.

I am not a doctor or a nurse, so I cannot advise you in medical matters. But personally, if I found myself in an area so remote that I knew help was at least twenty-four hours away, even by air, I might be inclined to take a gamble on using aspirin as a clot buster if I thought the stroke was likely due to a blockage, or I would try ibuprofen (Motrin or Advil) or some other anti-inflammatory medicine if I thought the stroke was the bleeding/swelling kind. I would try to make an educated guess which type of stroke it is because I know that the wrong choice of medication could make it worse, even kill! I would only do this in the direst of circumstances. It's a big decision because sometimes strokes are only temporary, clearing up themselves in a few minutes or in twenty-four hours, in which case it would be best to do nothing. These episodes are called transient ischemic attacks (TIAs). Therefore, I would wait fifty-nine minutes before I medicate.

I found several websites on the Internet that were highly informative regarding strokes, one of which is www.womensheartfoundation.org.

Super Smoothie
By Brenda Bush

2 handfuls of ice
1 frozen banana
1 handful of frozen fruit of choice
1 scoop of protein powder (optional) or douse
    with booze (optional)

Place all ingredients in a blender and blend well.

Sun-Dried Tomato Hummus
(A vegetarian meal)

By Brenda Bush

1 can garbanzo beans, drained
2 Tbs. tahini
sprinkle of soy sauce
salt and pepper
1/2 dozen sun dried tomatoes

Blend or puree all in a blender.

Linda Howarth gave us our own WWOW secret hand signal.

The W sign appears to be a cross between devil's horns and a tiara.

Linda demonstrates new ladylike finger gesture for the camera.

She was inspired at a WWOW gathering at Alabama Jack's on Card Sound Road one Sunday afternoon. It always rains in Homestead, and it rained so hard that it watered down the drinks, as Jack's shutters open *inward*, and they're six inches too short anyhow. But the rain did not dampen the enthusiasm of our WWOWzers!

Below: Hog Heaven, Windley Key.

Mexican Corn Casserole
(A vegetarian meal)
By Gail Feddern

Pam or other buttery spray

1 can white (shoepeg) corn, drained

1 can cream of corn

2 cans Mexicorn, drained

1/4 tsp. ground cumin

1/4 tsp. chili powder

salt and pepper to taste

1/4–1/3 C. salsa

1 bag of shredded Mexican cheese blend

2 slices of multigrain bread, toasted (Note: You can substitute Doritos, taco chips, or corn curls for the topping.)

1 Tbs. flour (Optional. Use if you want a firmer casserole. Cook 10 minutes longer if you use it.)

2 scallions, chopped
  (Non-vegetarian option: diced ham or Spam)

Preheat oven to 400 degrees. Spray a round glass casserole dish with Pam. Add corns, salsa, scallions, spices, flour (optional), optional ham or spam and cheese. Spray with buttery spray. Put casserole, covered, in center of oven. Cook at 400 degrees for fifteen minutes to melt cheese. Remove cover and crumble dry toast or scatter substitute on top. Cook five minutes longer.

Vegetable Compote
(A vegetarian meal)
By Gail Feddern

yellow squash (summer), sliced
green bell pepper, sliced
green scallion, chopped
small can tomato paste
salt-free Spike seasoning to taste
dried minced onion flakes to taste
black pepper to taste
water
Morton Lite Salt to taste after mixture is cooked

Cook all together in pan with cover for about five minutes or until done.

Pork and Sauerkraut
(A pressure cooker meal)
By Gail Feddern

2 lb. lean pork (spareribs, chops, or chunks)
2 large jars of sauerkraut, *rinsed*
1 C. water
2 Tbs. vinegar
1 or 2 apples, cored and cut up
pinch to 1 tsp. caraway seeds
1 to 3 Tbs. brown sugar or Brown Sugar Twin
    (Publix in Key Largo carries it or can get it.)
approximately 2 C. Hungry Jack potato flakes
    (Do not reconstitute.)

You may brown the meat first, if desired, but it's not necessary. Place the steam rack insert inside your pressure cooker, and put the meat on top. Dump sauerkraut and apple slices on top of meat. Mix together vinegar, water, brown sugar / Twin, and caraway seeds and pour on top.

Make sure the interfacing surfaces between the lid and the edge of the pressure cooker are wiped clean, then lock them together. Place the rocker knob where it goes on top of the lid, and put your closed-up pressure cooker on a stove burner on high heat to start it steaming, then lower it to medium heat and let it rock for 20 minutes. Turn off the stove. Using oven mitts or potholders, take the pressure cooker over to the sink and run cold water over the top of the lid until the pressure releases (the pressure indicator button will go down); if your pressure cooker has an additional switch to release any little bit of residual pressure, you may now turn it. The lid should twist off easily now. **Important:** *Always read the owner's manual instructions before using it the first time.* The above directions are for a simpler type of pressure cooker. Some of the newer models, such as mine, are quite sophisticated, with multiple safety features. But don't be afraid to use an older model.

Remove the steam rack. Fork in potato flakes. Serves 6.

Poor Man's Dinner

(A hurricane meal; can be a vegetarian meal)
By Gail Feddern

6 medium potatoes

2 medium large onions

1–3 Tbs. bacon grease, lard, Crisco, or vegetable/cooking oil

salt and pepper

water

catsup

Slice potatoes and onions. Heat shortening in a large skillet/pan on medium until it's hot but not smoking. Add potatoes and onions, salt, and pepper. Cook 5 minutes, turning frequently. (Tastes best if onions are crispy and potatoes are a little crusty.) Add enough water so that it doesn't burn, and turn ingredients over. Cover and turn heat down to simmer, turning ingredients occasionally until done.

Serve with catsup. Makes 2–4 servings.

Nesting ospreys.

Pennsylvania Dutch Fried Tomatoes
(A hurricane meal; a vegetarian meal)
By Gail Feddern

tomatoes, green and various stages of ripeness,
   including red
onions (optional)
flour
1 can evaporated (skim or whole) milk
shortening or cooking oil
salt and pepper

Slice tomatoes into approximately 1/4-inch-thick slices. Slice onions, if used, more thinly. Coat tomatoes with flour and salt and pepper.

Heat grease or oil in a large pan on medium heat. When hot, add tomatoes and onions. When crispy on one side, turn over and cook until crispy on other side. Add canned milk a little at a time; you want it to make a gravy, so use your spatula to turn ingredients, then cover pan and turn down heat to simmer. Check it frequently so that it doesn't burn. It's done when tomatoes are soft and the milk and flour have combined to thicken into a nice "white" gravy.

Tomato Garam Marsala

1 level Tbs. garam marsala (a Badia gourmet
blend spice [a Pakistan/India flavor])
2 large onions, sliced
olive oil
1 tsp. sugar (optional)

Basically, this is the same recipe as the previous but specifically uses the above ingredients. Serve it over rice, noodles, or toast.

Beef Stew

(A pressure cooker recipe)
By Gail Feddern

2 lb. beef stew meat (chunks of chuck or round or whatever)

8–10 carrots, rinsed, scraped, or peeled and cut into chunks

onions, an amount equivalent in volume to the carrots (Use small onions or cut larger ones into chunks.)

cooking spray, like Pam

1 large or 2 small beef bouillon cubes

1/2–1 C. of water (Note: you can substitute beef broth and omit the bouillon cubes.)

garlic or garlic powder (optional, but recommended if using round steak)

salt and pepper

dash of Worcestershire sauce (optional)

Spray the inside of a pressure cooker with the cooking spray.

Brown the meat in the bottom of the pressure cooker. Add the other ingredients. Put the lid on, pressurize, and cook for 20 minutes. Cook for 20 minutes if meat is fresh or thawed, 25 minutes if frozen. Serves 2–4 people.

Note: This is a low-carb recipe, unless you include potatoes.

Spaghetti with Pesto Sauce

(A hurricane meal; a vegetarian meal)
By Gail Feddern

1 lb. pkg. spaghetti or vermicelli
1/2 bottle extra-virgin olive oil
1–2 medium large onions, minced
1 whole scallion or wild onion top, chopped or
    1/8 C. dried chives
1–2 Tbs. Italian seasoning
4 large garlic buds, crushed and minced
1 tsp. salt
salt and pepper to taste
garlic powder to taste
condiments: grated Parmesan or Romano cheese

Bring water to boil in a large pot. Add tsp. salt. Break pasta in half and add to water. (**Note:** A few drops of olive oil added to the water will help prevent it from boiling over. A few drops of vinegar will make pasta carbohydrates less fattening, according to Dr. Oz!) Cook for 8 minutes.

While it's cooking, pour olive oil (and dried chives, to reconstitute) in a large pan. Add other ingredients and cook over medium heat until the onions are done. Drain pasta and combine all. Adjust taste, if needed, with salt and pepper, garlic powder, and additional Italian seasoning. Makes 2–4 servings. Serve with grated Parmesan cheese or Parmesan/Romano combo.

Man-Easy SOS
By Gail Feddern

4 handfuls fresh hamburger
1 level Tbs. dried minced onion
2 cans mushroom soup, condensed
1 can peas with half its liquid
salt and pepper
slices of toast
1 Tbs. butter (optional)

Pour pea liquid into a saucer and stir in onion flakes; let set to reconstitute onion. Put meat (and butter) in a pan and salt and pepper it. Mix in reconstituted onion with pea liquid. Cook on medium heat until done. Stir in soup straight from the can. Mix in peas. Heat mixture. Pour over toast and serve. Makes 4 servings.

Helpful Hint: To make an *emergency grommet*, push a smooth spherical pebble or coin into a piece of fabric from the underside, twist it so it forms a pouch, and tie the pouch off with a cord. Another method is to take a corner of the fabric, twist it, and tie it into a knot. Then tie a cord around the knot.

Both methods let you tie lines to pieces of fabric without harming the fabric.

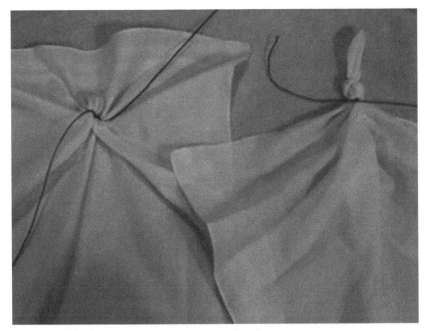

Left: rock grommet; right: knot grommet.

Ham Yellow Rice

(Can be a hurricane meal)
By Gail Feddern

2 Tbs. olive oil, separated
Pam cooking spray
one 10 oz. pkg. yellow rice mix
1 lb. canned ham
1/2 red bell pepper or dried equivalent
1/2 green bell pepper or dried equivalent
1 stalk celery, or equivalent in dried celery flakes
1 medium onion
water

Begin preparing rice. (If using dried vegetables, reconstitute in water.) While it's cooking, chop other ingredients. Spray large pan with Pam and add 1 Tbs. olive oil. Cook all ingredients except rice in pan, covered, for five minutes or until done. (You might need to add a little water to prevent sticking.) Stir in cooked rice and serve. Makes 7 servings.

Sloppy Joe
By Gail Feddern

4 handfuls ground beef/hamburger

salt and pepper

1 medium large onion, chopped (can substitute 1 level Tbs. dried minced onion flakes,
reconstituted)

1-4 sticks of celery, chopped (optional)

1 small can tomato paste

1 small can of water

1 heaping Tbs. Brown Sugar Twin (can substitute brown sugar, probably healthier but
more calories)

half-inch strip of prepared mustard (1/8 tsp.)

2 Tbs. Heinz catsup

dash of Worcestershire sauce

hamburger buns

Put hamburger and onion in a large pan, and celery
if used, and add salt and pepper. Cook over medium
heat until done. Drain away and discard grease.

While that's cooking, combine remaining ingredients in a bowl.

Add bowl contents to the pan mixture, stir,
heat, and serve over hamburger buns. Yum!

Gail's Low-Cal BBQ Sauce

Mix together the tomato paste, water, Brown Sugar Twin, mustard, catsup, and Worcestershire sauce from the previous recipe to make a delicious barbeque sauce good for pork, chicken, and baked beans.

You can ask Publix to get Brown Sugar Twin for you if you don't see it on the shelf, or you can order it online.

Stewed Tomatoes
By Gail Feddern

1 can of tomatoes
1 Tbs. sugar
1 Tbs. butter
salt and pepper
2 slices of bread

In a medium-size pot, over medium heat, heat first four ingredients until sugar and butter are melted. Mix in pieces of bread. Pour mixture into four saucers and serve as a side dish.

Note: You can "decalorize" this recipe by substituting Xylitol* crystals (from the health food store), stevia, or other sugar substitutes for sugar, Butter Buds powder and zero-calorie buttery spray for butter, and diet bread (I like Pepperidge Farms seven-grain diet bread) for regular white bread.

*Note: Never let your pets have Xylitol; it will harm them.

Wild Woman Vegetable Lasagna
By Cristine M. Pistol

1 pkg. of lasagna noodles
1 can stewed tomatoes with garlic and onion
2 bottles of spaghetti sauce with green and black
 olives (Clasico)
1 large tub of ricotta cheese
1 lb. of mozzarella cheese (sliced thin to medium)
1/2 lb. of provolone (thinly sliced)
one small bottle of Sazon (Badia seasoning)
2 bunches of broccoli
1 bunch of cauliflower
2 zucchini
1 bunch of carrots (grated lengthwise)
1 large onion (chopped)
1 red bell pepper (chopped)
 (green bell pepper optional)
1 Tbs. garlic (minced)
Parmesan cheese to taste

Preheat your oven to 350 degrees.

First cook the noodles as you would do with spaghetti, but make sure they are not fully cooked (they must have a little consistency to them). Spread wax paper on your counters, and as you take the noodles out, stretch them to dry on top of it. After you put the noodles to dry, we start with the sauce.

In a separate covered 5 qt. pan, mix the spaghetti sauce, stewed tomatoes, and chopped onion and peppers, and add the garlic. Season with Sazon to taste. Cook for approximately 20 minutes, stirring frequently. Wash and cut the broccoli, cauliflower, and zucchini.

Now you are ready to assemble the lasagna on a 9×13 lasagna dish. Cover the bottom of the dish with the noodles, making sure they overlap a little. Next, spread some of the broccoli, cauliflower, zucchini, and carrots over the noodles. With a ladle, pour some of the sauce over the vegetables, being careful not to move them. Open the ricotta cheese, and with your hands, play with it till you get a thin layer to spread over the sauce. Cover with slices of provolone and mozzarella cheese.

Repeat this process to make two layers or three if you have a deep lasagna dish. Your last layer should be sauce, provolone, and mozzarella cheese and Parmesan cheese to taste.

Cover and bake on 350 degrees for 45 minutes. Uncover and continue to cook for another 10 to 15 minutes. Take it out and let it sit for 5 to 10 minutes before cutting.

Enjoy!

A Little-Known Computer Tip: (OK, I'll admit it, I'm not very computer savvy, so maybe computer geeks all know this one, but it was new to me.) Betcha don't know what that little wheel in the middle of your mouse is for, do you? *Well, if you press down on the keyboard Control key while turning the wheel forward with your index finger, you'll see that it makes the print on your screen get larger!* Reverse direction to make the print smaller. A nice trick for us older, optically challenged people. It especially comes in handy for e-mail and print previews.

Note: You can do the same thing by holding down the Control key and pressing the + or minus key on the keyboard; the zero key returns it to normal.

Anne Baxter's Aunt Delsey Mae's Candied Yam Casserole

Yam Mixture
3 29 oz. cans of yams (sweet potatoes)
1 C. granulated white sugar
1 stick butter or margarine
1 tsp. salt
1/2 C. half and half or milk
1 tsp. vanilla

Topping
1 C. brown sugar
2/3 stick butter or margarine
1/2 C. flour
chopped pecans

Beat yam mixture all together and pour into a shallow dish casserole. In a separate bowl, mix together topping ingredients. Smear topping mixture on top. Sprinkle on chopped pecans. Bake at 350 degrees for 30 minutes, uncovered, until topping is a little bit crisp.

A CONTROVERSIAL FIRST AID TREATMENT – ELECTRICITY AGAINST VENOMOUS BITES AND STINGS

Can high voltage *low amperage direct current* electricity be used to save life or limb from venomous bites by some snakes, insects and spiders?

It would seem so, if you read British medical journal The Lancet, July 26, 1986, entitled "High Voltage Shock Treatment for Snake Bite" by medical physicians Ronald H. Guderian, Charles D. Mackenzie, and Jeffrey F. Williams. It told of successfully treating Waoroni natives that were bitten by venomous snakes in the Amazon jungles of Ecuador, who were hours away from a hospital where they could get antivenin. At first, they used electricity from an outboard engine, or whatever was available. For later cases, they had a modified stun gun, which put out **less than 1 milliampere of current at no more than 25 kilovolts,** using a 9-volt battery.

CAUTION—NEVER USE A/C HOUSE CURRENT TO TREAT BITES—IT CAN KILL YOU!!!

However, today most medical and government sources dispute the evidence. They say the snake bites were "dry bites," that the Indians survived because they were hardy enough to do so, that the snakes were not venomous, and that lab animals it was tested on died. These medical experts have no way of knowing those first three cases were true. They weren't there, and it is supposition on their part. As for the last, the small rodent lab animals are the natural prey of snakes and the venom kills them instantly, so there is no time to administer anything to them. Also, how exact was their duplication of a snake bite? (They used reconstituted venom, which could have been stronger than the natural. Did they take precautions with their hypodermic needles to guarantee not to inject deeper or more than a snake would?) Lastly, human beings are much larger and entirely different animals from rodents. The poison spreads more slowly in a human.

I sent an email to ron.guarderian@gmail.com and was pleased to receive a prompt reply from aleph.frackenthall@gmail.com, his son-in-law, who handles Dr. Guderian's correspondence. He said: "The information is just as valid as it was when it was published and there are just as many naysayers now as then." He went on to say "We always say using shock is first aid and should be done while on the way to finding medical treatment. When using a small engine, the spark plug wire is removed from the spark plug so the engine won't start. Just pull the rope or turn the car engine over. The spark plug wire is then held to where the bite is and the other side of the extremity is pressed to the ground. This should only be used on extremities."

Dr. Stan Abrams M.D. of Keene, Texas is another physician who has had great success using DC to treat venomous spider bites like black widow and brown recluse. I spoke with him over the telephone, and he still staunchly stands behind his findings. I strongly urge you to contact him yourself. His email is a001a@gmail.com. He will give you links for more complete information, documentation, history and origin. I found his data, especially case histories on the brown recluse spider bite, quite convincing. Click on Dr. Abrams' instructions and pictures using a modified stun gun applied to a brown recluse bite.

On a personal note, my husband Henry woke up with an ulcerated arm. Probably, a brown recluse spider bit him while he was sleeping. He went to his chiropractor, who treated him with his nerve-stimulating electric shock machine. The area healed nicely!

Note: Using electricity to treat venomous bites is controversial because of potential hazards if it's not done right, and it has not caught on with the medical community (which is very conservative by nature), so I must make this **DISCLAIMER: USE AT YOUR OWN RISK. DON'T FORGET TO CALL 911!** However, there is plenty of empirical and anecdotal evidence of its effectiveness. Here are some interesting websites with useful details if you wish to investigate further, to be prepared ahead of time in case of emergency. Google up the following: venomshock.wikidot.com. www.keelynet. com/biology/snake1.txt. www.rubyranch.us/pb/ wp. www.brownreclusespiderbitetreatment.com. I suggest you read both sides of the controversy and make up your own mind.

The following is an e-mail I received from my stepsister, Cathy. I don't know the originator, so I can't give them credit, but the subject line is

"Excellent Information for Safety." It's about tips to protect you against fraud. So here it is, as I received it.

This is very good information. Please make copies of it and share with others.

Attorney's Advice—No Charge

A corporate attorney sent the following out to the employees in his company.

1. The next time you order checks, have only your initials (instead of first name) and last name put on them. If someone takes your checkbook, they will not know if you sign your checks with just your initials or your first name, but your bank will know how you sign your checks.

2. Do not sign the back of your credit cards. Instead, put "Photo ID required."

3. When you are writing checks to pay on your credit card accounts, do *not* put the complete account number on the "For" line. Instead, just put the last four numbers. The credit card company knows the rest of the number, and anyone who might be

handling your check as it passes through all the check-processing channels will not have access to it.

4. Put your work phone number on your checks instead of your home phone. If you have a PO Box, use that instead of your home address. If you do not have a PO Box, use your work address. Never have your social security number printed on your checks (duh!). You can add it if it is necessary. However, if you have it printed, anyone can get it.

5. Place the contents of your wallet on a photocopy machine. Do both sides of each license, credit card, etc. You will know what you had in your wallet and all the account numbers and phone numbers to call and cancel. Keep the photocopy in a safe place. Also carry a photocopy of your passport when traveling either here or abroad. We have all heard horror stories about fraud that is committed on us in stealing a name, address, social security number, and credit cards.

6. When you check out of a hotel that uses cards for keys (and they all seem to do

that now), do not turn the "keys" in. Take them with you and destroy them. Those little cards have on them all the information you gave the hotel, including address and credit card numbers and expiration dates. Someone with a card reader or an employee of the hotel can access all that information with no problem whatsoever.

Unfortunately, as an attorney, I have first-hand knowledge because my wallet was stolen last month. Within a week, the thieves ordered an expensive monthly cell phone package, applied for a VISA credit card, had a credit line approved to buy a Gateway computer, and received a PIN number from DMV to change my driving record information online. Here is some critical information to limit the damage in case this happens to you or someone you know.

1. We have been told we should cancel our credit cards immediately. The key is having the toll-free numbers and your card numbers handy so you know whom to call. Keep those where you can find them.

2. File a police report immediately in the juris-
   diction where your credit cards were stolen.
   This proves to credit providers you were
   diligent, and this is a first step toward an
   investigation (if there ever is one). However,
   here is what is perhaps most important of
   all (I never even thought to do this):

Call the three national credit reporting organi-
zations immediately to place a fraud alert on your
name and social security number. I had never heard
of doing that until advised by a bank that called to
tell me an application for credit was made over the
Internet in my name. The alert means any company
that checks your credit knows your information was
stolen, and they have to contact you by phone to
authorize new credit.

By the time I was advised to do this, almost two
weeks after the theft, all the damage had been done.
There are records of all the credit checks initiated by
the thieves' purchases, none of which I knew about
before placing the alert. Since then, no additional
damage has been done, and the thieves threw my
wallet away this weekend (someone turned it in).
It seems to have stopped them dead in their tracks.

Now, here are the numbers you always need to contact about your wallet and contents being stolen:

1.) Equifax: 1-800-525-6285
2.) Experian (formerly TRW): 1-888-397-3742
3.) TransUnion: 1-800-680-7289
4.) Social Security Administration (fraud line): 1-800-269-0271

If you are willing to pass this information along, it could really help someone about whom you care.

Money-Saving Tip for Free Telephone Directory Assistance: Dial 1-800-FREE-411 (1-800-3733-411). Unlike 411 or 1-[area code]-555-1212, you won't be charged for the call, but chances are you *will* have to listen to a very short commercial message from one of their sponsors. So life's a trade-off—would you rather save time or money?

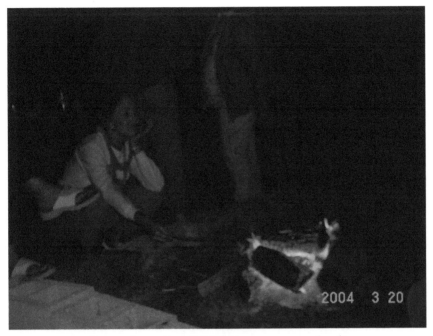

Just a bunch of Girl Scouts gone bad!

Helpful Hint: *Make wooden matches water-proof by dipping them in clear nail polish or melted wax.* If you use wax, melt it in a double boiler over water, *never* directly in a pot on a stove— or else it will catch fire!

WHAT A LOVELY BUNCH
OF COCONUTS

Coconuts might be your only source of water for a while. Coconut milk is watery, slightly sweet, and very nutritious. Plus, the meat is delicious and quite nourishing as it contains oil. You should try to find some coconuts. Coconut palms are frequently found between beach and jungle.

You might find good brown coconuts on the ground, but the coconuts most full of water are the green ones still on the trees. The problem, of course, is how to get them down. You can try to throw a grappling hook at them to pull down a bunch. Or build a ladder. Or grip the underside of the tree with your hands and walk up it one foot in front of another monkey-style like some tropical natives do, looking like a giant insect. Or hop up it froggy-style like other natives do. But you are not a native and probably don't have their strength, agility, and experience. There has to be a better way.

Towels tied together or clothing can aid climbing.

How to Climb a Palm Tree: Yes, you too can climb a palm tree! First, select a leaning palm tree. Face it so one side is sloping away from you. But to inch up a palm tree, you need to make aids for both your lower body and your upper body.

One way is to straddle the palm tree, using two rope circles tied around the palm tree's trunk. They need to be loose enough that they can be slid up the tree but not so loose that they fall down the trunk by themselves. On the lower rope, point your toes and slide the front of your right foot over the rope between the rope and the tree, and twist it one time so that you can lift the rope up to move it with the front of your foot; your heel is resting on top of the rope. Do the same with your left foot on the other side of the tree. Grasp the top rope, slide it up the trunk, then hold it in place and lift your feet and the lower rope up the trunk. Put your weight on your feet and again slide the upper rope as before. By alternating these actions, you can climb up, then down, the palm tree. Be careful not to let go of the top rope, or you might find yourself suspended upside down!

Another method utilizes a rope aid for the lower body too, but this one does not encircle the tree. Instead, it rubs against the *front* of the tree trunk. First, tie a circle out of some clothes or rope and lay it down on the ground in front of the tree. Twist it into a figure 8 and place your right foot in the right loop and your left foot in the left loop. Face the tree, grasp the backside of the tree with your hands and jump up it, pushing down with your feet. The arrangement around your feet provides the necessary friction to give you purchase. Progress up the tree in a series of jumps.

Actually, you don't need rope. You can wrap and secure just about any article of clothing around your feet. You can use a shawl, jacket, shirt, or pants. Wrap it around the instep and top of each foot and tie it, leaving an eighteen- to twenty-four-inch length or loop of cloth connecting your feet. The length depends upon the width of the tree's trunk. Similar to the figure 8 arrangement, this one looks more like a pair of manacles or handcuffs. The purpose of this fibrous loop is the same, which is to give your legs purchase against the trunk of the tree. You want to pad your feet to protect them and also give them a gripping surface for climbing.

If you don't have a rope or don't want to use clothing for this purpose, you can still climb a palm tree. If you are wearing a pair of boots with stout laces, undo the bows and tie each end of the shoelaces of one boot to the corresponding end of the other boot lace. (Leave the boots laced up as much as possible.) You end up with your boots connected together with two laces, and about eighteen to twenty-four inches apart. (Bear Grylls demonstrated this on a survival in the Everglades episode of Discovery Channel's *Man vs. Wild*.)

In the above methods, your toes will be pointed outward, one foot on the left and the other foot on the right side of the tree trunk, like a frog. You will jump on the front of the tree and push with both feet at once to climb up it.

Now that you've made an aid for your lower half, next you need to make an aid for your upper half. Tie one end of another article of clothing, such as a jacket sleeve, to one hand or wrist so you won't lose it.

Now to begin climbing: Stand at the base of the palm tree on the side that is leaning away from you. Reach your arms around the backside of the tree trunk, and grab the other end of the clothing that's attached to your other hand so that each hand has a firm grip onto the jacket (or whatever). Use your arms to hug the tree toward yourself. Then, hop up and place your feet on top of the palm tree trunk so that the length of clothing or rope on your feet is straddling it. Now move like an inchworm and climb that palm tree, pulling with the top half of your body and pushing off with your feet; grip with your knees while you release your arms enough to reach up for another hug of palm tree; grip, push, release, and reach, then grip, push, release, and so on, until you reach a cluster of coconuts.

Hang on to the palm tree's trunk with everything you've got except for one hand. You need a free hand to twist and pull off coconuts, hopefully by the cluster. Don't forget to get some immature green coconuts, as well as the ripe brown ones. Drop the coconuts on the ground. It's OK to climb among the palm fronds, and it's easier to harvest your goodies while resting on the top of the tree, but never put weight on the lowest fronds, because they are likely to give way. Instead, reach for the second, or better yet, third layer of palm fronds. While you're up there, consider taking some nice, green fronds for weaving mats, a hat, or building a shelter, but don't take the growing heart of palm,* a whitish green spear sticking straight up, because if you do, it will kill the palm tree. The brown cheese-cloth-like material found around the bracts of palm trees can be useful too as a crude strainer or a tiny seine for minnows along the shore. (One website suggested using this palm tree "wrapper" for toilet paper! *Ouch!*)

Come down the tree more or less in the same manner that you climbed it. Expect to get scraped up a bit until your skin toughens and you're used to it.

*Note: Hearts of palm are delicious, but I would hate to see you destroy a wonderful coconut palm and all its potential for the shortsighted pleasure of having a salad for lunch! Better to sacrifice a cabbage palm, or try using palmetto, which are plentiful.

Warning! Climbing up and down palm trees or any other tree is inherently dangerous. Attempt

at your own risk. Practice going up and down short distances on short trees first.

There is another method, but it's slow and laborious. It's froggy-style but employs ropes with Prusik climbing slings. It offers three-point security, a rope for the hands, and one for each foot.

The advantage of the **Prusik knot** is that it is quite stable. Under load, it will not slip, yet you can move it when it's no longer under tension. I suggest you learn this knot well as it can also be very useful in various survival situations, allowing you to climb even straight trees, pipes, ropes, and vines.

My impression is that a Prusik knot is really no more than a multiple girth hitch drawn tight.

How to make a Prusik Knot:

1) Tie a circle of rope together using a secure, slip-proof knot. (Many climbers recommend some variation of a fisherman's knot.)
2) Put the circle behind the tree trunk.
3) Going through the other loop, wrap the knotted end around the trunk two or more times. The more wraps, the better it grips.

The fewer wraps, the easier it is to push the finished Prusik knot up or down.

4) Pass the knotted end through the standing loop, and *pull back*.

5) Keeping the wraps parallel, pull on the knotted end to tighten.

6) You've made a **Prusik knot!**

See the illustration to learn how to form a Prusik knot sling.

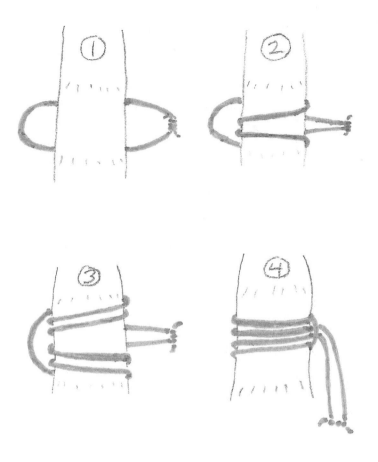

To summarize: Pass the knotted end through the loop to form a girth hitch. Go around again two or three times. Dress the coils and tighten. The Prusik knot is finished. Move it up by grabbing below the Prusik and pressing upward, or on top and pressing down to go down. To loosen, open up the loop with your thumb.

You'll want to make three of these Prusik knot arrangements—the highest one in the center for your hands, one on the right for your right leg, and one on the left for your left leg. First make one to hang from the right side of the tree. The tied-off ends should form a loop and be the proper length for your cocked leg so that when you put your right foot in it and stand up in this "stirrup," it will give your body a boost up. Next, make the same arrangement for the left side. Finally, make one in the center of the trunk and above the other two; attach it to the front of your belt. This last one is used to pull yourself up and steady yourself while you manipulate the slings for your feet. To move up the tree, simultaneously lift one foot and, with your hand, move the Prusik knots up another step, and then bear down with your weight on that leg. Alternate your legs. For example, move the center sling and left sling up. Bear down on the left leg. Move the center sling and the right sling up. Then shift your weight onto the right sling. Repeat the sequence.

How to Open a Coconut: Sharpen a stout stick by whittling it to a point with a knife or something else with a sharp edge. Fire-harden it by turning it slowly over a fire until it is brown and won't dent under your fingernail. Stick it in the ground so that the pointed side is up. Pound it into the ground (before you sharpen it) or bury it in the sand, but it must be fixed securely to work. The exposed portion must be at least a coconut's length high. Gripping a coconut with both hands, pound it down against the stake. Do this repeatedly, peeling the tough husk away bit by bit, until you've freed the nut inside. An easier method is to do the same thing on a broken branch of a low-growing or fallen tree. You might have to sharpen the branch first.

Save the fiber from the husk as it has many uses also, such as an aid to starting fires, burning as a "smudge pot" to repel mosquitoes and sandflies, an aid in filtering water, bedding, floatation, cordage, etc.

Next, take another sharp instrument (knife, ice pick, sharp stick, or pointed end of a shell, like a conch whorl) and puncture two of the three "hole" depressions found on the end of the coconut that loosely resembles a monkey's face (as opposed to the pointed end of the coconut). One hole is to pour out the milk, and the other hole is to break the suction to facilitate this. Use the juice. When it's empty, crack the coconut against something hard and remove the meat; if necessary, use a shell or knife to do it. The unripe young coconuts contain a delicious custard-like gel.

You can render coconut oil from copra (mature, sun-dried, or smoke-dried coconut meat). Shred it, boil it, let the water cool, and then skim the oil off the surface. Coconut oil has a reputation for soothing sore skin. You can use coconut oil in cooking, e.g., frying and sautéing; in addition, a tablespoon or so of coconut oil added to food imparts a nice flavor. You can pour it in a seashell or a coconut shell, add a fiber wick, and you have a lamp for a source of light or a portable source of heat. Or dip torches in it.

Save pieces of coconut shell, too. You'll find them useful for implements: scrapers, cups, bowls, boiling pots, ladles, etc.

The coconut palm is indeed an amazing tree, functioning to save lives and provide comfort in a variety of ways.

Gail's Shrimp Creole
By Gail Feddern

2 lb. raw, headless shrimp, in the shell, not deveined
2 C. or 2 medium large onions, chopped
3/4 C. green bell pepper, chopped
3/4 C. red bell pepper, chopped
1 C. or 2 sticks of celery
1 Tbs. olive oil
2 small cans Hunt's tomato paste
2 small cans shrimp water (the secret ingredient!)
2 bay leaves, large, or Old Bay seasoning
1 tsp. salt or Tony Chachere's creole seasoning
hot pepper sauce
2 C. of cooked rice

Boil shrimp with salt and 1 bay leaf in water to cover for 5 minutes or until shells turn pink. *Do* not *throw away the water the shrimp was boiled in!* Instead, remove the shrimp without draining away the water; when the shrimp is cool enough to touch, peel and devein the shrimp, *throwing the peelings/ shells and scraps back into the pot of shrimp water.* Prepare rest of ingredients.

Put oil in a large pan and sauté celery, bell peppers, and onions until celery is tender and onions are transparent but not browned. Stir in tomato paste. Get a metal screen strainer. Stir up the pot of water and shrimp scraps and strain out 2 cans full of the water. Add the cans of shrimp water and 1 large bay leaf to the mixture in the pan and stir until blended. Stir in the shrimp, cover, and simmer a few minutes, stirring occasionally. You want it thick but not burned; you may add more shrimp water if necessary. Serve over rice. Makes 5 servings.

Note: You can add dashes of hot sauce and creole seasoning before serving, or let your guests suit themselves. Remember, hot sauce gets hotter each time it's heated—but you probably won't have leftovers anyhow!

Note: This is one of those meals that tastes even better the next day, so make it the day before you plan to serve it.

Gail's Shrimp Gumbo
By Gail Feddern

1.5 lb. raw shrimp in the shell, not deveined
1 lb. fresh okra or 1 pkg. thawed frozen okra,
    cut into 1/2-inch pieces
1/2 C. celery, minced
1 C. green bell pepper, minced
1 C. onion, minced
1 clove of garlic, minced
1 can of minced tomatoes
1 can chicken broth or shrimp water
1 C. rice, cooked
2 Tbs. butter (may substitute other fat or oil)
2 Tbs. flour
2 bay leaves, separated
2 tsp. salt, separated
1/4 tsp. pepper
2 tsp. gumbo filé
hot sauce to taste, at table

Peel and devein the shrimp and set aside. Put the shells and scraps in a pot with water to cover, 1 tsp. salt, and a bay leaf, and boil for 5 minutes. Pour it through a wire mesh strainer; this is your shrimp water. You can use shrimp water in cooking the rice, if you like.

Make a roux with the butter, celery, onion, garlic, bell pepper, and flour, stirring frequently. Sauté until celery is tender or for 5 minutes, adding a little liquid as necessary. Add a bay leaf, crumbled, and season with salt and pepper. Add a can of tomatoes and a can of chicken broth or shrimp water combination. Simmer covered about 30 minutes. Add okra and raw shrimp to the mixture and simmer covered another 5–15 minutes. Stir in 2 tsp. filé. Mix in cooked rice, or ladle gumbo over bowls of fluffed rice, and serve. Better yet, refrigerate it overnight and serve it next day hot.

Note: You may substitute chicken, fish, or other shellfish.

WHAT TO DO IF YOU ARE
MAROONED ON A MANGROVE KEY

In addition to the main inhabited keys of the Florida Keys, there are a great many smaller uninhabited mangrove keys located throughout Florida Bay. It's a popular area for fishing, so it's not an impossible thought that you could someday find yourself swimming for the nearest one because your boat sank or through some other misfortune.

Most mangrove keys got their start from floating mangrove seedlings washing up on spits and sand bars and taking root. Flotsam and jetsam make it easier for more mangrove seeds and seedlings to lodge and grow amongst the trash. After a period of years, a tiny mangrove island forms. I have personally witnessed this. As time goes on, the little key just gets larger. There are about four different kinds of mangroves—red, white, black, and buttonwood. Black mangrove and buttonwood like higher ground. Usually you'll find red mangrove growing in the saltwater, their almost angular prop roots arching down into the water, crisscrossing each other and forming a nearly impenetrable barrier. Frequently attached to the roots are thin but edible coon oysters. Also, mangrove crabs with amphibian lifestyles scoot around the mangroves.

Some mangrove keys have "iron shores" (fossilized coral rock), but even those keys might have a sandy side. You should walk or wade around your little island and explore it. To ward off sunstroke while doing so, I suggest you weave yourself a hat from palm fronds, or piece together one from sea grape leaves, or see if you can find a vase sponge to fit your head. (I once saw a hippie on Money-Penny Key, looking like Robinson Crusoe, wearing a vase sponge hat. He first dried it out to kill itchy critters like hydroids; after it was cured, he wet it down and put it on his head. It cooled his pate by evaporative air conditioning.) If you find a sandy shore, set up your camp there above the high tide mark.

As you approach, little fiddler crabs may rush away en masse, perhaps disappearing into holes in the sand. But they are not hard to catch. Except for the shame-faced crab, most crabs, even small ones, are a food source (but cook before eating!), as well as good bait. You might also find hermit crabs on the shore or on higher ground, maybe amongst sea purslane and other weeds, or in the center of the island.

Rattlesnakes, especially pigmy rattlers, occur in the Keys. They can swim, so you might come across one on your wild key. It's a good idea to cut for yourself a long forked stick from a sapling, six feet long, or whatever length you can handle comfortably. You don't want the fork too long, because the purpose of it is to pin the snake to the ground, just behind the head. Also, if the gap in the fork is too deep, the snake will wriggle out from under. Trim the ends of the fork to 1 or 1½ inches long. You want the fork gap to approximate the thickness of the rattlesnake. This doesn't matter so much if the ground is soft, because you can still pin him down, but it's critical if you are trying to hold him down against hard rock. I wouldn't attempt to capture him if he's coiled up, because you don't know how far nor how high he can leap to strike! If he's coiled, stand at what you think is a good safe distance and chuck rocks at him. When he slithers off, run up behind him and pin him down with your stick. If you have him pinned securely, you can then reach down and grab him behind the head to control him. Cut his head off, or smash his head with a rock to kill him. Do *not* try to kill him by holding his tail and swinging his head against a rock! His poisonous fangs would probably scratch you in the process, and you'd be in *big* trouble! Even the dead head can harm you, so bury it deep enough so you won't accidentally step on the fangs. After he's dead, skin him and clean him, and cook him for dinner. Rattlesnake is said to taste like chicken.

Frequently, the interiors of these little islands are "bald" with sand or perhaps even limestone coral. Additional species of crabs might reside there. Sometimes the interior of a key offers a swampy haven for water birds. Rainwater collects in the solution holes or pockets of this hard coral surface. Although it may be fresh, that doesn't necessarily mean that it's safe to drink without boiling or distilling it first, because you'd be sharing it with birds, rats, or other germy critters.

It's best to boil this water before drinking; if you don't have a metal container, look around the island for a tin can or aluminum can or soda can to use for a pot to boil it in. You can make a fire if you find a glass jar, clean it up, fill it up with clear water, and put it in the sun. If conditions are just right, it will magnify the sun's rays, and you can use it like you would a magnifying glass to start a fire. Best chance is around noon on a hot summer's day; arrange tinder around the bright focused spot; allow air to circulate; when it starts to smoke, blow gently until it bursts into flame. Wood from a mahoe or sea hibiscus tree, century plant, and driftwood are supposed to be good materials for making fire via friction. (More on making fire later.)

It's a judgment call if you have no means of purifying water. It's common wisdom that a person can live only three days without water. Drinking water that is infected with disease organisms can make you violently ill. You would become weak, feverish, and dehydrated from vomiting and diarrhea. If you do get sick, in dire circumstances one can ingest charcoal from a campfire because charcoal carbon is a purifier. When you are mashing it up to make a paste to add to your food or water, be careful not to get it into your lungs. I remember reading once that charcoal from a campfire saved the life of a World War II POW whose buddies were dying of dysentery. If you think this might be a future concern for you, ask a pharmacist for more information. Of course, it is hoped that you would be rescued within three days, but there are no guarantees. *Remember, never drink saltwater. It will kill you. Guaranteed. Boiling or filtering saltwater does* not *make it safe to drink.* To be made potable it has to be distilled, which might be done by boiling, but only the *condensation* is safe to drink.

Your best chance is to try to attract attention to your plight. If you filed a float plan, search planes will come looking for you. Spell HELP (or the international distress signal SOS) in letters at least six feet wide on a clear spot on the beach above the high water line. If you can, do the same for the bald spot in the middle of the key. Use whatever materials you can find to contrast against the background, for example, deep wide impressions in the sand, or pile rocks or coconuts. Also, three bonfires in a triangle is an international distress signal. Rubber or petroleum products added to a fire makes thick, black smoke; burning fresh-cut green foliage produces gray smoke. Look in the trash washed up in the weed line for things you can use; I'll bet you'll find at least one rubber flip-flop you can burn to make a dense signal fire. Soda pop cans or maybe even an old CD, either of which (with a little work) might reflect the sun enough to use for a signal mirror.

Passing boaters can see vertical structures easier than horizontal ones, so drape clothing or something against the mangrove trees. Dying mangrove branches would present a color contrast against the living green foliage, but it would take a few days to turn yellow or brown. Tie your shirt or something else to a stick or branch to wave as a flag for help because you need something broader than your arms for people to see from a distance.

Sound carries well over water if the wind is blowing in the right direction. You are lucky if you know how to do that two-fingers-in-the-mouth whistle because it is very shrill! If not, maybe you can blow a conch shell horn. I'll tell you later how to make one.

If you happened to have a spool of monofilament fishing line and a box of cereal, cookies, crackers, or some other snack with an inner bag made of Mylar, you could try to make a kite and fly it. Or perhaps with a piece of cloth or some other wick material soaked in diesel fuel or kerosene, you could make a Chinese flying lantern. (These mini hot-air balloons were used in ancient times for communication during battles.) Mylar makes a dandy radar reflector. Once, when my daughter was little, we tied a Mylar helium balloon on a one-thousand-foot spool of 10 pound test nylon monofilament fishing line and let it fly up. In short order I received a phone call from Homestead Air Force Base! If it doesn't work out as an aerial signal, hang on to that

Mylar anyway; even a small strip from a candy bar wrapper can be used to attract fish.

If you get hungry while waiting for rescue, you can forage for food in tide pools. Small fish, mollusks, sea urchins, sea cucumbers, and crabs make their homes there, and most are, to some degree, edible. Even if you have fire, you might prefer to eat many "sushi-style" to benefit from their raw moisture. But survival expert Bear Grylls warns that raw crab is full of bacteria and should always be cooked before eating. You can crush crabs and larger seashells with a rock. However, do not eat the shamefaced crab, because I read that it is poisonous to eat. If you don't have a hook or thin stiff wire to pluck the tiny tidbits of meat from bleeding tooth nerite seashells, then use a thorn. Chances are good that there are some thorny vines, bushes, or trees on the island. You can also fashion fishhooks from those thorns.

The century plant is a tall plant with a single stem growing out of a base of long succulent leaves, each leaf tipped with a thorn; large white flowers cluster around the top of the central stem. The central stem makes an excellent twirling spindle for friction fire starting, especially if the other fire board is mahoe. Thorns on the century plant, while not suitable for fishhooks, make good sewing needles as the thorn is already attached to the "thread." Pounding a leaf from a century plant will reveal lots of these threads that can be used individually for fishing line or twisted together into sisal rope. Indian Key is loaded with century plants, which were planted long ago by Dr. Henry Perrine, the historical botanist.

Lures can be made from sisal, feathers, hair, fur, brightly colored leaves, and pieces of shells, especially if they're colorful or reflective. Plastics, metals, and food wrappers you find can work, too.

Fishhooks are not mandatory for catching fish. You can make a gorge. A fish gorge is a small piece of wood sharpened on each end and grooved in the middle for the fishing line. After wrapping a line around the middle a few times and tying it off, bury the gorge inside a chunk of bait. (A clam found in tide pools, under a rock, or in the sand or mud along shore will catch the first fish; thereafter you can use pieces of fish for bait.) A fish swallows the bait, and provided the gorge is perfectly balanced and the right size, when you pull on the line, the gorge turns sideways and lodges inside the fish's mouth or stomach. Keep tension on the line while you pull the fish out of the water. You can also use fish bones for hooks. You can sharpen and fire-harden a stick or sapling to spear fish and octopuses. If you were going to be there a while, you could consider nets and fish traps.

Did you know that you can eat those ugly sea cucumbers? Inside sea cucumbers are flat strips of white muscle that run lengthwise. That's the edible part. Shores, tide pools, and shallow water can provide you gastronomical adventures you might never have tried before. Many Japanese people like to scoop out the roe of sea urchins and eat it. They are also big fans of seaweed of different varieties. I don't know of any poisonous seaweeds; there may be, and I just don't know about it. But I have personally eaten two ounces of raw *Sargassum* seaweed at a time without any ill effects whatsoever. Provided you had enough freshwater to drink, I would think it would be a good idea to eat seaweed to keep your digestive tract operating properly. It's bound to be full of vitamins and minerals that your body needs, as other edible seaweeds are. Sea purslane growing above the shoreline is rich in vitamin C too, so there is no excuse to get scurvy! Look for cactus plants as well. The ripe fruits, after the minute prickers have been gingerly rubbed off with a piece of cloth or something or charred off, are not only nutritious but delicious!

Swim around your island and look for a triton trumpet under a rock or a horse conch or queen conch lying on the sandy or grassy bottom. Although I wouldn't eat the triton trumpet because it uses toxic acid saliva to paralyze and digest its prey, it's shell makes an excellent blowing horn; just be cautious cleaning it. Horse conch and queen conch are edible, and you can make loud horns from the empty shells. (Incidentally, triton trumpets and horse conchs are carnivores; they eat other shells and crustaceans. Triton trumpets especially like starfish, and horse conchs like sea biscuits and sand dollars and queen conchs. Queen conchs, on the other hand, eat algae.) If you find one, check to see if it has legs. If it does, then it's a hermit crab that has appropriated an empty shell.

I once met a couple from California who told me a funny story. They were new to South Florida. They had heard that conch tastes like abalone, which was a favorite of theirs back home. One fine day they were walking above the high water mark at Crandon Park Beach on Key Biscayne, when they spotted a "queen conch" just crawling along on top of the sand. Dinner! They took it home, killed it, and cleaned it. They threw away the claws. They boiled and ate "that sausage thing," which they said tasted *terrible*! They didn't think much of our "conch"!

Well, of course, it wasn't a queen conch at all, just a large hermit crab inhabiting a queen conch shell. Queen conchs always stay in the water, but some hermit crabs propagate on land, so that should have been their first clue. The second clue was that conchs don't have claws; they have an operculum foot, with which they pull themselves along the bottom of the ocean. Ironically, my new friends could have eaten the hermit crab's claws, but they had discarded that only edible part and had eaten the intestines instead!

Incidentally, you can get a hermit crab to abandon its shell if you pour Coca-Cola into the shell.

If you do find a real, live queen conch, knock off the first three or so spirals from the pointed tip. This is necessary both to make the mouthpiece for your seashell horn and to release the animal so you can ease it out. If it's very stubborn, you can tie a cord around its fleshy foot and hang it from a tree branch or clothesline; eventually, the weight of its own shell will overcome its muscle strength. Or you can hang the shell and set a container of seawater underneath it, allowing the creature's foot to just touch the water to encourage it to come out. It may take days. Yes, I know it's an unbearably cruel thing to do, but remember you are in a life-or-death survival situation. (When it was legal to take queen conch, I put the whole shell in my chest freezer, which quickly and humanely killed it. The next day after thawing it, I could pull the whole animal carefully out, without even damaging the shell.) You can eat it raw. The meat will be tough unless you tenderize it by pounding it or rubbing papaya sap or juice on it or wrapping it in papaya leaves. It's delicious, especially with a little juice of a Key lime sprinkled on it. Even the tough foot is quite tasty raw with just a little Key lime juice on it. To remove any vestiges of animal tissue left in the shell, lay the shell face down on an ant hill for the ants to eat, or put it back in the sea face up for the little fish, shrimps, and crabs to clean up. Once it's clean, if you knock the tip off, you can use it for a horn. To form the horn's mouthpiece, you must remove the first three spirals from the tip of the shell. (You can do this by hitting it with a rock or another conch shell.) Looking at the mouthpiece, it should be a smooth, pink funnel and a hole; if not, you might need to remove some internal spiral structure to make it work right, but try blowing it first. You blow on it like a trumpet. Pick up the shell and hold it with your hand wrapped around the smooth, curved natural opening that the animal came out of. Purse your lips, press them against the hole in the spiral end, and "give it the raspberries!" In other words, make a *brrrrrrrrrrt* sound with your vibrating lips. Keep practicing; eventually you will get it. The sound is very loud and deep, and carries a long way—a mile or more.

Hopefully, someone will hear or see you and be curious enough to investigate something unusual and come to your rescue. You can even sound out SOS on the horn (three short blasts, three long blasts, three short blasts).

Helpful Hint: Go to the library or buy a book on the local flora and fauna. (Learn to weave coconut fronds too.) You'll learn which are useful or edible, which ones to steer clear of, and which ones are protected. There are some trees that can be very helpful. For example, along the Stretch (U.S.1 between the Keys and mainland Florida City; it cuts through the Everglades), you can find willow bushes. Willow bark tea was the original aspirin. Early Keys settlers made an **infusion of gumbo limbo bark**** to counteract the dermatitis caused by brushing against a poisonwood tree. Leaves from a Jamaican dogwood / fish fuddle tree crumbled up and thrown in a tide pool is said to kill fish because it contains rotenone. Besides helpful plants and trees, you need to learn which ones to avoid, such as the terrible manchineel tree. Carib Indians tipped the stingray barbs of their millet reed arrows with the poisonous sap. Indians tied their enemies to manchineel trees; they'd be crazy or dead by morning. All parts of this tree are bad. Even smoke from burning manchineel wood is highly irritating or toxic. The tree looks innocent and inviting. The fruit looks like small green or yellow apples, smells good, and tastes sweet. But don't try it! After a moment or two, you will probably feel a burning sensation in your mouth, and your throat may swell shut. The corrosive effects might not start right away, but when they do, they are serious, possibly deadly, and may require gastrointestinal surgery! So learn all you can about the local plants and trees in the Keys.

Ditto for animals. Learn which animals (and trees or plants) are protected. Some animals are dangerous or poisonous. Some are not, and some are edible. Exotics are generally not protected, but be cautious; also, be sure not to break any laws.

Iguanas are colorful and weird looking. I used to hand-feed Mr. Iguana bread and bananas when he visited our sea wall—until a friend told me her husband had to have his finger surgically removed after his pet iguana gave him a necrotic bite!

When I was in the Yucatan peninsula, I saw a man standing by the side of the road holding a dead iguana by the tail. My guide told me the natives there eat them. I understand you can catch them with a long-handled net.

Iguanas and other exotics are gaining a foothold in Florida. While some may be stowaways, unfortunately, too many pet owners disobey the law and release their exotic pets into the wild because they've grown too big or they're tired of them. Some exotic releases have been unintentional, a consequence of hurricanes. The photo you've probably seen of the large dead alligator partially swallowed by an even larger dead snake (probably an anaconda, but possibly a boa constrictor or a python) is not a hoax. It was taken in the Everglades and witnessed by a park ranger.

**Anti-Itch Formula:*

1/4 C. gumbo limbo bark
2 C. water (distilled, if possible)

Scrape bark from the gumbo limbo tree, both bronze outer bark and some green inner bark.

Boil water. Add bark shavings. Turn off heat. Let steep for 20 minutes. Soak a paper towel or a clean cloth in it and apply to skin.

Helpful Hint 1: *Get relief from the pain of sunburn by gently dabbing on vinegar.* If you're the patient, you won't mind the strong odor, because you'll immediately feel better!

Helpful Hint 2: *Cut a leaf from an aloe plant, slice off the thorns, peel it, and gently rub the gel onto the skin.* Aloe is famous for treating burns.

A WWOW TALE OF THE AMAZING RED SHOES

WWOW'S magic red dancing shoes raring to go—
they just won't let Merlot rest even a minute!

"Oooeee! Deese shoes sho' is killing me! Ah wisht ah'd nevah laid eyes on dem. But as soon as ah seen dem, ah just gots to get dem. Dey sho is purty, dough, ain't dey?" The voluptuous woman in a red satin dress three sizes too tight nudged her companion, who nodded in agreement.

She hobbled a few steps more down the cruise ship corridor. Then, "Well, ah cain't take dis no mo!" She leaned against her friend and took the feathery red high heels off her swollen, blistered feet.

A group of our WWOWzers happened to be strolling along behind her on the Promenade Deck of the Carnival cruise ship. "Will you take twenty bucks for them?" asked CZ.

"Sold!" was the reply. And the exchange was made.

It wasn't until later, at one of the ship's dance bars, that the secret properties of the beautiful red shoes were revealed. Amazingly, the shoes would fit any WWOW member who put them on! (Original owner notwithstanding.) A little anesthesia supplied by the bartender and applied by mouth had the desired numbing effect, and regardless of shoe size, all our girls could dance in them. The other remarkable thing was that when the shoes heard salsa music, they automatically began dancing. Even if the person didn't know how to dance to Latin music, the shoes did it for her. And the shoes kept on dancing, not letting the WWOWzer sit down and rest unless another WWOWzer was waiting to dance with the shoes. And thus the night was danced away, the Wild Women on the Water and the gorgeous red shoes having a wonderful time.

Malaysian Fruit Salad
By Tanya Feddern-Bekcan

Brown Sugar and Lime Syrup:

1/4 C. light brown sugar, lightly packed (Regular brown sugar would probably be too sweet.)

Grated rind and juice of one large lime or lemon (Use more or less if you wish to substitute Key limes—try to grate the colored peel and not the bitter whitish skin underneath.)

2/3 C. of water

Fruit Salad:

1 large can (20 oz.) of pineapple chunks in pineapple juice, (not syrup so the pineapple won't be too sweet)

1 large can (15 oz.) of Libby's Tropical Sliced Mango in light syrup (if getting another brand, do not choose green mango)

1 large can (15 oz.) of Libby's Tropical Chunky Papaya Mix in light syrup and passion fruit juice (if getting another brand, do not choose green papaya)

1 can of pitted lychees in light syrup

Add the light brown sugar, grated lime/lemon rind, and juice to the water in a small saucepan. Stir with a wooden spoon and heat gently at medium heat until the sugar is dissolved. Raise heat to medium-high or high heat until it boils, then turn it down to simmer for about a minute. Remove the saucepan from heat and let it cool.

Open the canned fruit and drain out the juice/syrup in the cans. Put the mango slices on the cutting board or plate and cut them into bite-size chunks with a paring knife. Put the pineapple, papaya, lychees, and mango chunks into a serving bowl. Pour the cooled brown sugar and lime syrup over the fruit salad in the serving bowl. Cover with plastic wrap and cool in the refrigerator (or put in a cooler filled with ice) before serving.

Oyster-Flavored Sauce and Vegetables over Beef-Flavored Rice
By Tanya Feddern-Bekcan

First Group of Ingredients:

3 Tbs. of peanut oil

4 green onions, cut into 1/2-inch pieces

6 slices of peeled fresh ginger root (Slice off a piece of ginger root that's about 1 inch in diameter by 1/4 inch thick—then cut it into 6 slices lengthwise and then cut them in half widthwise.)

Second Group of Ingredients:

1/2 C. beef broth

1½ Tbs. oyster sauce (found in the ethnic section of most grocery stores)

1½ Tbs. soy sauce (you can substitute low-sodium soy sauce)

1/2 Tbs. of cooking sherry or cooking wine

2 tsp. of cornstarch

2 tsp. of sugar

several drops to 1/4 tsp. of sesame oil (found in most grocery stores)

pinch of pepper

Third Group of Ingredients:

1/2 lb. of cleaned mushrooms (sliced or you can use small whole mushrooms)

2 C. of broccoli cut in bite-size pieces (you can slightly blanch it in boiling water first, if you wish)

12 sliced carrots—cut in circles about 1/4- or 1/8-inch thick (you can slightly blanch them in boiling water first, if you wish)

Rice:

1½ C. rice (to yield 2 C. of cooked rice)

2½ C. of beef broth

1 tsp. salt

pepper

Rice—Cook This First

Put the rice, beef broth, and salt in a saucepan and season with pepper. Stir and heat on high heat until it reaches boiling point, then cover with tight-fitting lid and cook on medium-low heat for about 15 minutes or until cooked.

Main Dish

Heat the wok with peanut oil at medium-high heat. Add in the green onion and ginger root and heat until fragrant (a couple of minutes), stirring frequently. Add in the second group of ingredients (beef broth, oyster sauce, soy sauce, cooking wine/ sherry, cornstarch, sugar, sesame oil, and pepper). Continue cooking and stirring it until the sauce becomes bubbly. Now, add in the third group of ingredients (mushrooms, broccoli, and carrot) and turn the heat to medium-high. Stir vigorously with a wooden spoon or spatula for several minutes. Don't worry, the veggies will shrink and there will be plenty of sauce! Now, raise the heat to high heat for several minutes while continuing to stir vigorously until the vegetables are lightly cooked. You don't want the vegetables mushy, but you probably don't want them too crunchy either. Serve over the rice.

ABOUT STINGRAY BARBS

Tourists are cautioned to shuffle their feet when they go wading in saltwater to give stingrays lying on the bottom fair warning that someone is coming, so please get out of the way. You definitely don't want to step on a stingray! At the base of its tail, a stingray has a hard boney barb that can easily pierce through the sole of a tennis shoe or rubber boot. This barb has many tiny backward-pointing serrations on both edges, and it's covered with a toxic slime. The early Indians in this region fastened stingray barbs to the ends of reeds for their arrowheads. If you are ever wounded by a stingray barb, you will never forget it because the pain is excruciating!

Helpful Hint: *Running **hot water** (**not scalding!**) on a stingray wound is the only thing that will take away the pain—temporarily!*

A stingray made the news worldwide when one killed the famous crocodile hunter Steve Irwin. About two weeks later, an eighty-nine-year-old man in Florida was also pierced in the chest by a stingray, *yet he did not die!* Why not? Why did the young man in magnificent physical condition die and the very old, presumably much feebler man survive? Philosophies aside, let's examine the facts. Steve Irwin instinctively immediately pulled out the barb, thereby allowing the blood to gush out of his heart. He was dead in a couple of minutes. The old man, on the other hand, kept the barb in his chest. Probably he broke it off, someone did it for him, or perhaps the struggling stingray broke it off. In any case, *the barb acted as a cork to plug his heart.* He was rushed off to the hospital that way and surgeons were able to save his life. *Whether it's a stingray barb, a knife, ice pick, or sharp road debris, resist your natural inclination to withdraw the object from the wound because doing so will cause even more, sometimes fatal, damage to the person!* Instead, secure the penetrating object to the body as best you can so that it can't move, or at least as little as possible, and rush to the hospital to let an expert medical team take care of it. It's moot as to whether Steve would have made it or not.

A Life-Saving Reminder from Sylvia Miles, of Sea Bird Marina: Never get out of your boat without being sure you can easily and safely get back in again.

- Don't forget to throw the anchor! First, make sure it is securely tied to the boat. Tie it in a figure-8 knot on the bow cleat.
- Anchor off the bow. Point the bow into the waves and toss the anchor, tines in the downward position. When it hits bottom, pull a little to set it. Place the anchor line in the starboard or port bow chock.
- Don't anchor in coral. That's illegal because it damages the coral. If you can see bottom, aim for a white patch, which denotes sand. Coral looks brown.
- Avoid anchoring the stern to prevent pitch-poling or waves coming over the stern and swamping the boat.
- After anchoring, wait for your boat to swing around and come to rest before you think about going into the water. Turn off the engine, or at least put it in neutral.
- Assess the situation. Is it a mud bottom? How shallow is it? You don't want to drown in quicksand or get stuck in muck or hit your head. (One large man was mired in

muck up to his waist; fortunately, another boat happened along and rescued him.) Is there a current running? Is there wind blowing hard? Are current and wind going in the same direction? (Sylvia told me about a man who drowned while swimming after his boat.) (Note from author: A drifting boat is mostly affected by wind because most of its bulk is above the waterline. A person in the water has only his head above the water; his bulk is largely underwater, so he is most affected by water current.)

- Attach your boat ladder securely to your boat so that it won't accidentally come off. Are you sure your ladder or dive platform is adequate for you to get back into the boat by yourself? If not—stay in the boat!

What to do if you are in the boat and someone is in the water, but a strong current is preventing him from getting back into the boat: Quickly let out a lot of line so that the slack will nullify the effects of the current long enough for the person to climb aboard. It's all relative, like a stuntman in the movies jumping from one vehicle to another while both vehicles are traveling seventy-five miles per hour. It can be done only as long as there are no differences in their speeds. Even though both vehicles are traveling very fast, their *relative* speed (to each other) is zero. If the person in the water is not at the transom of the boat or close to the stern, you will most likely have to hoist anchor, or untie or cut the anchor rope and drift back to him if he is directly behind the boat. If you have to release it, first tie some flotation to the anchor line so that you can recover your anchor line later. If the person is not in line with the boat but a ways behind and to the side, then you will have to motor over to him and pick him up; just be sure to put the gear in neutral when you approach him.

If the person is missing and you must go looking for him, do this:

- Note the time; write it down, if possible.
- Mark the spot where you were. Activate the Man Overboard feature on your GPS.
- If you are anchored, tie a boat cushion or bumper to the boat end of the anchor line, unhook the line from the boat, and throw the line and cushion overboard. This will mark the starting point for your search.

- If you are not anchored, throw an unattached boat cushion overboard to serve as a guide as to where a lost swimmer might move with the current.
- Motor over to neighboring boats to see if they've seen him.
- Begin running a transect of the area using your float as a starting point if there's no trace of him. At the same time, call the Coast Guard.

Important, Potentially Life-Saving Tip: *How to stop a runaway boat.* Speed your boat ahead of the runaway boat and turn and drag a floating rope across its path. The rope will foul the propeller and stop the boat.

Boater's Mnemonic:
Brown, brown, run aground.
White, white, you just might, but anchor right.
Green, green, good to go.
Blue, blue, cruise on through.

ANCHORING
By Henry Feddern

As a general rule when anchoring, let out enough line to equal three times the water depth. If anchoring in a current or in rough seas, let out more line, for a 5:1 ratio if you have it. My anchor line is two hundred feet long.

I recommend six feet of chain between the anchor and the line. This helps the anchor to hold onto the bottom and prevents the line from chafing on rocks.

The chain should be naked stainless steel. At one time I used a plastic-coated chain, but one day the chain broke apart because the plastic concealed corrosion of the chain.

The shank of the anchor should be in the form of two parallel rods connected by an inverted U at the top, with a slip ring, such that the ring can slide from front to back of the shank. The anchor chain is attached to the ring. The ring, by being able to slide forward of the flukes when driving the boat forward beyond the anchor, unhooks the anchor from the bottom without bending the flukes or damaging the bottom. Shanks that only have a hole at the end for attaching the chain can only be freed from the bottom by levering the flukes upward, thus breaking whatever they are hooked into or bending themselves.

When anchoring, avoid corals. Sanctuary regulations state that it is illegal to anchor on corals when they can be seen from the surface. After anchoring, if there is any doubt about the presence of corals, it is best to dive down to the anchor and move it, the chain and the line, away from touching the corals. At this time, you can also place the anchor so that it will hold well but also can be retrieved when you want to move the boat.

When retrieving the anchor, lift the line out of the bow chock, but leave the line attached to the bow cleat, and motor forward and slightly to the side of the line until you are well beyond the anchor. If you motor directly over the line, the motor might wrap the line around the propeller.

Put the boat in neutral, and then quickly pull in the line—the anchor's ring should slide forward and release the flukes from the bottom. If the anchor doesn't release, then rapidly release and pull tight the line several times (the chain will pull the line down and possibly release the anchor). If the anchor still doesn't release, let the line go and repeat the procedure but motor in a slightly different direction. (The chain or line might be caught under something.)

As a last resort, turn off the engine or put it in neutral, then dive down and unhook the anchor yourself. Grabbing the anchor, pull yourself up the anchor line. Throw the anchor into the boat and climb aboard. Pull in the rest of the line. You can also use the engine to power forward and break the anchor free, but usually you will end up with a bent anchor. You can straighten the flukes, but usually, modern anchors are so poorly welded that the welds will start to crack. When this happens, it is safest to buy another anchor.

If you are in a current, motor forward slowly while touching the line alongside the boat until you feel the line suddenly become looser. This means the anchor has disengaged from the bottom. Put motor in neutral. Pull the line up quickly before the current hooks the anchor again.

Knowing how to properly deploy and retrieve an anchor is basic boatmanship. I rarely have to buy an anchor because I find so many of them on the bottom—anchors that other people left behind.

(Note from wife, Gail: I saw a boat anchored under a bridge that had its anchor line running through a hole in a float. I complimented the captain for his ingenuity. He said he hasn't lost an anchor since. The sea bottom under Keys bridges is littered with debris and anchors. Whether you improvise one like he did or buy an anchor retrieval system, it is a good idea to have a float on your anchor line not only to make it easy to pull your anchor but for safety's sake. If you have to cut your anchor line in an emergency, you can tie off the float to the line so you can come back later to recover your anchor.)

Broiled Fish with Gail's Turmeric Fish Sauce
By Gail Feddern

1/8 tsp. turmeric powder

4 rounded Tbs. mayonnaise (I used Hellman's light.)

2 fish fillets (I used porgy and it turned out good!)

1 Key lime

Cut Key lime in half. Squeeze juice of 1/2 Key lime on both sides of fillet. Repeat with other fillet. Marinate 5 minutes. Prepare sauce by mixing turmeric with mayonnaise in a small bowl. Pat fillets dry, both sides. Place fillets on a broiler pan. Spread sauce on fillets. Put pan of fillets under a broiler and cook 3 or 4 minutes or until browned slightly. Turn fillets over and spread remaining sauce. Cook the same way until done. Flesh should be white, not translucent, but with clear juice. Yum! Serves 2.

Pralines
By Sylvia Miles

2 C. sugar
1 C. brown sugar
1 stick butter
1 C. milk
2 Tbs. Karo syrup
4 C. pecan halves
1/2 tsp. of vanilla or almond extract

Add all ingredients except the butter and cook until it begins to bubble. Stir constantly until it thickens and begins to turn to sugar. Add butter. Drop onto waxed paper.

Matecumbe Mahi
By Cindy Strack

8 mahi-mahi fillets
1 C. flour seasoned with seasoned salt
2 eggs, beaten
Japanese bread crumbs seasoned with Old Bay,
    salt, pepper and garlic salt
cooking oil
Sauce:
1 C. mayonnaise
1/4 C. Dijon mustard
hot sauce, a few drops

Dip fillets in flour, then egg, and finally the Japanese bread crumbs.

Heat oil in large fry pan over medium heat. When hot, put in fish. Cook about 4 minutes or until brown. Flip fillets, and while second side is browning (about 4 minutes), brush browned side with sauce. When second side has browned, flip once again, and when all are turned, take off heat and put on serving platter. Serve extra sauce on side.

THE MALFUNCTIONING SCUBA REGULATOR

By Gail and Henry Feddern

My husband, Henry, and I are fully licensed marine life fishermen legally operating out of our home. We live in a stilt house, with his saltwater tanks of critters under the house. While he catches some fish, he's made his reputation in invertebrates, so most of the tanks are full of crustaceans and gorgonians. There are gaps under the doors downstairs, so amphibious critters skittle around and creepy crawlies come and go at will. I keep my face mask downstairs. I have a problem with cockroaches (or something!) chewing on my silicon face mask. I tried keeping my face mask upstairs, but you go out diving and forget your facemask just once, and that's the end of that! I theorized that cockroaches nutritionally needed the silicon for their wings, so I left an open can of silicon grease near my dive bag for them to chow down on instead. It seemed to work for a while, until the silicon grease ran out. So now, I just periodically replace my facemasks. They get moldy in that damp atmosphere anyway. I find that cockroaches seem to prefer the clear silicone facemasks to black silicone face masks. As for my regulator, before my dive, in addition to checking the air pressure, I always purge the mouthpiece to blow out any possible cucarachas, scorpions, centipedes, or millipedes before I take a breath.

Henry had just gotten his regulator back from the shop, where it had been overhauled. He and I were out in the boat and made our dive inshore in shallow water. No sooner had he entered the water, when he felt something hard protruding from the mouthpiece, and the airflow was restricted. What was it? Was it a loose piece of hardware the repairman forgot to tighten? He pushed on it with his tongue. It receded, and he could now breathe normally.

Back in the boat after the first dive, he looked over his regulator carefully, but couldn't find anything amiss. So he went down again.

Again, he felt something inside his mouth. Was it a tie-wrap touching his tongue? *What the heck was that thing?* He boldly gripped it with his teeth and lips and pulled! He looked to see what it was. No, it wasn't a tie-wrap. And no, it wasn't a roach either. He was surprised to see a little mangrove crab swimming madly for the bottom! Evidently, it thought it had found the perfect home in Henry's regulator.

After the crab's departure, his regulator breathed smoothly again.

Eggs Parmesan
By Gail Feddern

Simply add 4 good shakes of grated Parmesan cheese to each egg you scramble or for omelets.

Speedy Chicken Cacciatore
By Pat Rosendale

one 9 oz. pkg. refrigerated angel hair pasta
olive oil–flavored cooking spray
one 18 oz. pkg. frozen cooked diced chicken breast
1 green bell pepper, cut into 1-inch pieces (about 1 C.)
1 small onion, cut into 1-inch pieces (about 1 C.)
one 15 oz. can chunky Italian-style tomato sauce
2/3 C. water
1/4 tsp. pepper

This recipe works well with leftover chicken.

Cook pasta according to package directions, omitting salt and fat.

While pasta cooks, coat a large nonstick skillet with cooking spray; place over medium-high heat until hot. Add chicken, green pepper, and onion; sauté until chicken is browned and vegetables are crisp tender. Stir in tomato sauce, water, and 1/4 tsp. pepper. Reduce heat and simmer uncovered 5 minutes, stirring often.

Place 3/4 C. drained pasta on each of 5 plates; top each serving with 1 C. chicken mixture. Yields 5 servings.

Shrimp and Feta Scampi
By Pat Rosendale

1 (8 oz.) pkg. spaghetti
1–1/2 lb. peeled, deveined large shrimp
1 (10 oz.) pkg. frozen snow peas
4 green onions, sliced
1/3 C. olive vinaigrette
1/4 tsp. freshly ground pepper
1/2 C. crumbled feta cheese
water

Bring 2 quarts water to a boil in a large sauce-pan. Add pasta and cook uncovered 9 minutes.

Add shrimp to pasta; cook uncovered 3 minutes or until shrimp is pink. Place snow peas in a colander. Drain pasta and shrimp over snow peas to warm.

Transfer mixture to a large serving bowl. Add onions, vinaigrette, and pepper; toss lightly. Sprinkle with crumbled feta cheese. Yields 4 servings.

This meal is very easy and not very time-consuming. If you purchase already peeled and deveined shrimp, it can be prepared in under 15 minutes. If you purchase unpeeled fresh shrimp, you'll need to purchase 2 lb. in order to end up with 1½ lb.

Deep Dish Pizza Casserole
By Pat Rosendale

1 lb. ground round
one 15 oz. can chunky Italian-style tomato sauce
cooking spray
one 10 oz. can refrigerated pizza crust dough
1½ C. (6 oz.) preshredded part-skim mozzarella
 cheese

Preheat oven to 425 degrees.

Cook meat in a nonstick skillet over medium-high heat until browned, stirring until it crumbles. Drain if necessary and return to skillet. Add tomato sauce and cook until heated.

While meat cooks, coat a 13×9 baking dish with cooking spray. Unroll pizza dough and press into bottom and halfway up sides of baking dish. Spread meat mixture on the pizza dough but not on the sides.

Bake uncovered at 425 degrees for 12 minutes. Top with cheese and bake 5 minutes or until crust is browned and cheese melts. Cool 5 minutes before serving. Yields 6 servings.

LOVE ME TINDER

To be successful in starting a fire you must start small and build up. The order goes tinder, kindling, twigs or chips, sticks, and lastly logs. The finer the tinder, the better it is. Actually, just about anything can catch fire if it's fine enough, it has many surfaces, and the conditions are just right. Ever hear of a silo or grain elevator fire? The fine dust from grain can explode!

Bet somebody that you can make steel burn, and you will win the bet. Here's how: Take a roll of plain steel wool, 00 or finer, and ignite it with a match or spark. It burns! In fact, you can use a hunk of steel wool and two flashlight batteries as an emergency fire starter. Unwind a strip 1/2 inch wide from the steel wool pad long enough to span two "D" batteries end to end. Hold the batteries together vertically (positive to negative). Press one end of the steel wool against the bottom (negative end) of the first battery; with the other hand, brush the other end of the steel wool strip against the top battery's positive terminal (button end). It will spark and catch on fire, and you can use it to start your tinder aflame. I learned this trick from the book *Roughing It Easy* by Dian Thomas (ISBN 0-8425-0892-9). **Note:** I have since learned that just about *any type of battery will do. A single 9-volt battery works easiest—just rub it across steel wool!*

Make a tinder bundle resembling a bird's nest to receive your hot ember. Good sources for tinder are the following:

- lint from your clothes dryer lint trap
- thin papery outer bark from trees, like gumbo limbo and *Melaleuca*
- newspaper or paper, preferably shredded up fine
- scrapings or shavings from dry wood or inner bark
- fire fungus (a certain fungus that grows on birch trees up north)
- charred cloth
- untreated hair from humans or fur from animals
- "monkey fur" (Extract it from a palmetto plant by twirling a stick in the bract of a

frond. Watch out for stinging insects like scorpions, poisonous spiders, etc.!)

Not classified as tinder but helpful aids in starting fires are as follows:

- resinous sap from a true pine tree, such as are found on Big Pine Key and the mainland. (Australian pines are not real pine trees!)
- beeswax
- paraffin
- flammable solvents. (Be careful of gasoline—it's very dangerous because it's *explosive*! It's best to avoid using it.

Judy O'Hara-Vetrick, WWOW's camping guru, offers her recipe for "candle kisses." Take old, broken, or used candles and cut them into 1-inch pieces. Wrap each piece in *wax* paper. Use them as aids to start campfires.

Light My Fire!

There are many ways to start a fire. Mother Nature sometimes creates fire through lightning, volcanoes, or spontaneous combustion of a pile of oily rags, natural gas, oil, coal, peat, and even a decomposing compost pile. Man, however, doesn't want to depend on serendipity; he wants to make a fire when he needs it. That's why most people start fires with matches or cigarette lighters. In a primitive situation, modern man may feel at a loss if he suddenly needs to build a fire and he finds himself without matches or a lighter. However, his options for creating fire are just as good as Mother Nature's, but he still needs her cooperation, as well as his own skill. The basic essentials that fire needs are oxygen, fuel, and heat. With a match or a cigarette lighter, you have all three essentials in a tiny package. In a primitive environment you can probably find fuel, and you are surrounded by air, so the missing element that you need is heat. The various ways of achieving heat are friction, compression/percussion, electricity, solar energy, spark, and chemical reaction.

The purpose of this book is to make you aware of knowledge you need in a survival situation. It is far beyond the scope of this book to go into great detail about how to make fire by the many different methods. (Go to other books or the Internet for specifics.) If you know the basics, then you can be creative. Don't be afraid to adapt something for another use. Think first of the different types of fire heat. Then look around you to see if there is anything in your environment that can be made to produce enough heat to start a fire.

- Friction: fire hand drill, bow drill (an improvement over the previous), pump or flywheel fire drill (best of the three), fire cord (pulling a cord or vine through a notch or knothole), fire plow, and fire saw
- Compression/percussion: fire piston, gun, flares, and striking stones or iron or steel together to produce heat or sparks.
- Electricity: shorted AC house current or battery
- Solar energy: focusing the sun's rays through a lens (magnifying glass or parabolic reflector)
- Spark: electrical or mineral (as in percussion)
- Chemical reaction: sudden oxidation of a liquid, gas, or powder, or by combining substances

Now let your imagination run wild! Although you probably don't know how to do it, you've heard of rubbing two sticks together to make a fire. And you might have known little boys who played God by incinerating ants with a magnifying glass. But did you know that you can make a fire using wood alone, *rocks, iron or steel, ice, a balloon or condom, a broken light bulb, a soup ladle, a measuring spoon, a wine glass, Saran wrap, a soda bottle, a Coca Cola can and a Hershey bar, the wrong end of a pair of binoculars, hand lotion, and contents from a first aid kit?* Surf the World Wide Web for fire making, and you will be amazed at what you will find. For example, some of my favorite websites are **camp-firedude.com, wildwoodsurvival.com, primitive-ways.com, and fieldandstream.com** (look up an article titled "Seven Ways to Start a Fire without a Match"). **YouTube** has a lot of good fire-making demonstration videos. All these websites will teach you the different procedures to start a fire.

If it's a sunny day, ask yourself, "What can I use to make a lens to harness solar energy to make a fire?" A convex lens is needed. That's something round or spherical. Eureka! How about a drop of water on your glasses? A balloon or condom or Saran wrap filled with water might work! You'd have to twist it tightly to force the water into forming a sphere and thereby stretching the material into transparency. Or even a clear light bulb with water, or a wine glass, but you might have to cover it with

Saran wrap to keep the water in when you tip it to focus it. Or a capped clear plastic soda bottle, or clean jar with water in it to concentrate the sun's rays into a hot spot on tinder.

In freezing temperatures, you can shape an icicle, stack and shape thin ice from a brook, freeze water in a bowl, or tie up and freeze water in a section of waterproof fabric to make a sphere of ice; the only criteria is that the ice be roundish and clear. (To protect your hands from the coldness and to slow down the ice's melting, it's best to hold it by a strap wrapped around once.) *Yes!* Even ice is capable of making fire!

A concave, parabolic reflector will also focus the sun's rays enough to make fire. The criteria here are that it must be a polished, reflective surface. You can use a stainless steel mixing bowl, a soup ladle, a measuring spoon, and yes, a soda pop can whose bottom you've polished with a bit of chocolate bar and wrapper (or perhaps seaweed or coconut husk).

Check out first aid kits and cosmetic bags. If you find potassium permanganate and glycerin, you can start a chemical fire. Sprinkle the crystals on the tinder, then pour on a little glycerin (you can substitute glycol antifreeze); after several seconds it will ignite.

Note: These items are good to have on hand, but obviously must be kept separate from each other in their own leak-proof containers. If you are trying to make a fire by friction, you can make it easier if you combine a little potassium permanganate and *sugar* in the "sweet spot." I read that three crystals of potassium permanganate in 1 liter of water (turns light pink) will purify drinking water, but wait half an hour before drinking it. A bit more (turns purple) is said to be a good antiseptic and antifungal treatment. It can also be used on snow as a purple stain to attract attention. Glycerin, we women know, softens our skin.

You need to generate eight hundred degrees of heat to cause a fire. Primitive fire making is as much an art as it is science because there are a lot of variables, and it's the fire maker's judgment call as to how to control those variables. Except for lenses, your materials must be perfectly dry. Usually, your tinder should be shredded finely to expose multiple surface areas to oxygen. The hardness or softness of the wood, stone, or metal is crucial. You have to apply a lot of vigor to produce a lot of sparks or enough heat when using percussion and friction methods. The proximity of the tinder is important. The tiny, burning coal requires quick and careful handling. Charred cloth or fungus tinder are the most promising to catch and nurture an ember initially.

Chicken Breast
By Daryl Stone

4 chicken breast, split
3 to 4½ oz. dried beef
1 can cream of mushroom soup, mixed with 1
C. sour cream

Cover bottom of pan with beef, lay breast on beef, cover with soup and sour cream. Bake 3 to 3½ hours at 275 degrees, uncovered.

Lobster Bisque
By Daryl Stone

Steam lobster in rice cooker. Use the antenna and any other lobster meat. Not tails. Save tails for special meal.

lobster meat scraps
1 tsp. onion, chopped
4 Tbs. unsalted butter
6 Tbs. flour
1 quart of milk

1/4 C. dry sherry
1/4 tsp. celery salt
salt and pepper to taste

Sauté the lobster and onion in butter for a short time.

Remove lobster and set aside. Sprinkle flour over butter and onion, add milk, and stir until liquid thickens, about 10 minutes, stirring constantly. Add lobster meat and stir in sherry and seasoning.

MEMO TO WWOW MEMBERS
From Gail Feddern
Regarding Scary River Adventure

Maybe not all of you know who got into trouble at the annual camping kayaking trip this year (2006). It was me. I darn near died! If it weren't for my daughter Tanya Feddern and my friend Cristine Pistol and her crewmates Diane and Sheri, I probably would have drowned or been eaten by alligators (maybe both!). So I would like to publicly thank them for saving my life.

For those of you who weren't there, I didn't know how to make a portage with my kayak. I *still* don't know the correct procedure, so if one of you knows how, please e-mail me instructions because I'd better learn how, so I'll be ready for next year!

Anyway, to make a long story short, I tried to launch myself and the kayak together from the incline of the wooden portage. It might have worked too if I'd had my feet on the foot braces, which I couldn't find and had assumed were missing but were actually just very high, just below the lip of the cockpit and not on the floor where I expected them to be! I went down the incline *inside* my kayak and ended up on my back, with my feet in the pointy end and the back of my head hitting the edge of the seat. The kayak lagged momentarily behind, then launched itself and started to capsize, but I quickly rolled my weight to the other side, and it righted itself, getting only a gallon or two of water inside the cockpit. However, the kayak with me lying there looking helplessly up at the canopy of trees was drifting out into the current. I couldn't scoot myself up to a sitting position because there wasn't room to bend my knees, and my hands and forearms were at the wrong angle and insufficient to gain purchase on the rim of the cockpit. I could maybe paddle, but as those of you who were there know, the Loxahatchee River is merely creek-wide in spots, full of sharp bends, fallen logs, stumps, and snags. (Did I mention alligators? We didn't actually *see* any, but park rangers warned us to stay out of the water. I wondered if some of the things our vessels slid over were really gators slithering underneath us!) In any event, there was no way I could navigate while in that position. I needed outside help fast!

Now just a few feet away from it, Gail and kayak were headed right for that dam—with its four-foot waterfall! Thank God for Tanya and Cristine's quick actions! Tanya jumped into her kayak and raced alongside me to head me off from the dam. Without regard to her own life, she thought only of saving her mom. She could have been swept over the falls too! While she held me off, Christine and friends turned my bow.

From my point of view, I had a very narrow perspective of what was happening. I do remember Sheri hollering for me to hang on to that tree to keep from being swept away. There was a big cypress tree to my right with a bunch of knobs on the trunk. I reached out and grabbed onto knobs and hung on for dear life.

I am told that they got me to the opposite bank. Cristine reassured me and told me to rest, to let my strength build up while they brainstormed. Everybody gave their verbal input to solve the problem. Then somehow, between Cristine's canoe and Tanya's kayak, they maneuvered me back across the river to the portage. There Cristine and Tanya both left the security of their vessels and stood waist deep in tannin-brown water to try to help me. Tanya straddled my bow while she and Cristine tried to pull me out. Girls, you *know* I ain't no feather! I weigh almost as much as the two of them put together. I remember Cristine on the wooden portage, her

GAIL UNDERWOOD FEDDERN

arms reaching down for me, I see her extending her dominant left wrist in a soft black cast because she had a broken or dislocated bone, and I was thinking, *Oh, man, that's gonna hurt*, and would I cause permanent damage? But she insists, "Just *grab* it!" She said, "Gail, you are my friend, and I am *not* leaving you here!" Between Cristine and Tanya's determination, adrenaline, and the strength of my guardian angel, they got me out of that kayak. I think part of the rescue operation involved me hanging onto some overhead branches clad with Spanish moss while they slid my kayak forward.

PS: After I was once again safely ensconced in my kayak and hadn't paddled very far, I saw a triangular-shaped piece of driftwood with scaly looking bark lying on the water against the bank about 6 feet away from me. Was it a piece of pine with a knothole, or could that knothole be a big ol' alligator's eye with the nictitating membrane covering his slit pupil to fool me? I wasn't about to poke it with something to find out.

Lessons learned:

1) First, before I do something, I should learn the right way to do it.

2) **We should break up into roughly three groups where there isn't room enough for the entire group.**

3) These groups should **keep in contact with each other**—either by cell phone, marine radio, or whistle, by whatever means of communication that circumstances dictate.

4) Every WWOW member should wear a whistle or horn clipped on a cord to her vest. A good, pea-less plastic whistle of 120 decibels or higher costs $3–$6 and is well worth the price. I and my rescuers did not have the time or hands available to grab a whistle and blow, but if Diane, the middle passenger in Cristine's canoe, had a whistle, she could have blown an SOS of three short, three long, and three short blasts to summon help.

5) It was a good idea that the leader of the event passed out small slips of paper with the participants' cell phone numbers on it. Unfortunately, the list was incomplete, probably because some participants failed to turn in their cell phone numbers to the leader in time.

6) It makes no sense to take your cell phone with you and not have it turned on! It certainly doesn't make it more waterproof to have it turned off. (If you're worried about it getting wet, get one of those floating containers or dry bags specially designed to keep your cell phone safe from moisture— or at the very least put it in a Ziploc bag.) OK, you don't want the civilized world disturbing your commune with nature, I can understand that. Just hang up. Or if you *must* turn your phone off to get any peace, at least check your messages every ten minutes. *Don't* wait until you have reached your destination!

7) **If a group has stopped along the way to wait for the rest of the group to catch up, and some members are still missing after fifteen minutes, initiate a phone call, radio call, or whistle signal to the missing participants. Don't *wait a half hour and then continue on!* If *after twenty minutes* nobody has seen or heard from them, then something is probably wrong, so *you need to go back and help them.* Send two vessels of able-bodied women back to**

look for them. Be sure to keep in communication with the rescuers. If possible, keep the rest of WWOW subgroups informed of what's going on, especially the leader of the outing.

8) **Upon departure and return, a minimum of two vessels of able-bodied WWOW women should hang back to see that all the girls are safely launched onto the water.** Tragedy can strike as easily at a private or public dock as well as on a wild river. Let's adopt these **rules for safety** so that in future outings we Wild Women on the Water can have even more fun 'cause we'll be carefree, knowing we have a good plan in place!

—Gail Feddern

M y Heroes! Cristine (L.) and Tanya
(R.) at dangerous portage.

A scene on the beautiful but scary Loxahatchee River.

Possible Life-Saving Tips: How to get away from an alligator. Most people know not to swim in and to be super cautious around bodies of freshwater in Florida and other parts of the Deep South as they are quite likely to contain alligators. Alligators are extremely dangerous animals, and they are much stronger and faster than you. They can leap five feet or more out of water and run at least thirty miles per hour! They have powerful tails with which to knock you down. They are sneaky. They can stay underwater for twenty minutes if moving, but for several hours if lying still. They can lie or creep just below the surface of the water, with only their nostrils and eyes exposed; they look like a log floating or a snag. They seize their prey and roll around with it in order to drown it. If it's a large animal too big to gulp down in a few bites, like a deer or a *human*, they will take it to the bottom and shove it under something for it to decay so they can eat it later. Because of alligators' tremendously strong jaws lined with large teeth and the pathogens in their mouths and surrounding water, most people who are attacked by alligators don't survive, and if they do, they are usually severely maimed.

If an alligator has you in its jaws, *gouge or strike it in the eye* with all your might! If your hand is inside its mouth, but you can still move it a little, try to **pull its throat flap** to drown it; maybe with your other hand you can do it by pulling on loose skin under its chin. **Bite or punch its nose.** (You can try to hypnotize it by stroking its underside like the Indians do, but it probably won't be in the mood.) Try any of these things. If it releases, even momentarily, which it might do to get a better grip before it rolls you, break free and swim for safety as fast as possible! Your best bet is to get to shore and run away at a zigzag; alligators have short legs, so they cannot change direction easily. Report it to Florida Wildlife Conservation Commission (FWC) and seek medical attention immediately.

Alligator.

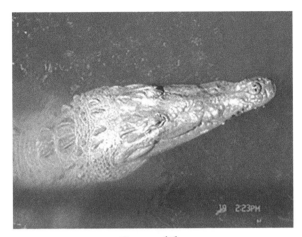

Crocodile.

Predominantly, alligators live in fresh water and crocodiles live in saltwater. Alligators are blackish and have broad snouts and heads. Crocodiles have narrow snouts. Unlike crocodiles in some foreign countries, the crocodiles that live in Florida are reputed to be shy. There is a crocodile sanctuary in North Key Largo, adjacent to Card Sound Road, and just south of the Ocean Reef Club.

Cream of Mushroom Soup
By Phyllis Williams

1½ lb. chopped fresh mushrooms
1 small onion, grated
4 Tbs. butter
4 Tbs. flour
1 tsp. salt
1/8 tsp. black pepper
4 C. milk
2 C. chicken stock
1/4 C. sherry
1/4 C. fresh parsley, chopped
barley (optional)

Cook mushrooms and onion in butter until golden brown.

Blend in flour and seasoning. Add milk and stock. Cook until slightly thickened, stirring constantly. Add sherry. Serve and garnish with parsley. Makes 6 cups of soup.

Note: If you want barley, add 1/2 C. barley and 1/2 C. water and simmer for 1/2 hour.

Italian Spinach Casserole
From Phyllis Williams

2 lb. ground beef
1 medium onion, chopped
one 15 oz. can tomato sauce
one 12 oz. can tomato paste
2 tsp. basil
1 tsp. white sugar
1/4 tsp. pepper
1 tsp. brown sugar
1 tsp. oregano
1/2 tsp. minced garlic
1/2 tsp. thyme
two 10 oz. pkgs. frozen chopped spinach, thawed
1 lb. cottage cheese
8 oz. mozzarella cheese, shredded

Brown the meat and onion. Add tomato sauce, paste, sugars, garlic and seasonings. Bring to a boil. Reduce heat to low and simmer, uncovered, for 10 minutes or until thick, stirring often.

Squeeze out as much liquid as possible from the spinach. Combine spinach and cottage cheese, using a fork.

Evenly spoon the meat mixture into a 9×13 pan. Sprinkle with half the mozzarella and top with spinach mixture. Sprinkle top with remaining mozzarella.

Bake uncovered at 375 degrees for 30 minutes or until hot and bubbly.

Enjoy!

DIVER'S SURVIVAL EQUIPMENT

Maybe your boat sank, the dive charter left without you (as in the movie *Open Water*), your boat floated away without you because it dragged anchor or the anchor line broke, or you got swept away by a strong current, sudden tide change, or rip current.

If you are a diver who finds herself adrift in the ocean, Lake Okeechobee, or other large body of water, and you've done all you can to help yourself, but you're still in trouble, *you are a diver in distress*, and you need to summon *help* fast! It can happen to any of us. Your best chance for survival is to *be prepared beforehand—carry a personal rescue kit*. Don't go into the water without it.

You are at the point where you must depend upon somebody else to save your life. First, they have to notice you; second, they have to know that you want them to come and get you; third, they have to realize it's a serious life-or-death emergency and that they need to *act now!*

A diver adrift in the ocean has about three days to live, realistically speaking. The biggest concerns are dehydration and sharks. But others have survived even greater odds, and so can you.

You need the means to be able to attract attention during daylight, darkness, and anytime.

Daytime Signaling Equipment

1. **Sea Sausage**—an inflatable tube that you hold vertically to signal for help. It's especially useful for waving at nearby boats. When not in use, it is rolled up. I recommend that you replace the flimsy plastic clip that comes with it with something more substantial (e.g., a bronze snap-swivel or stainless steel D-ring).

2. **Folding Dive Flag**—sections of white PVC tubes that are spring-loaded with bungee cord, with a small dive flag attached to one end. Unlike the sea sausage, which can fold over in a stiff wind, this device is stiffer and narrower, so it stays erect better. It's not a distress flag, so it can be used in everyday diving so your buddies in the boat can locate you. It makes a 3×10 inch package,

with a loop of the bungee cord at one end for attachment.

3. **See/Rescue Streamer**—a six-inch-wide by twenty-five-foot-long orange floating plastic ribbon with the international distress symbol of black ball and square at the end; it is periodically reinforced with plastic sticks to keep it from twisting. You attach one end to yourself and unroll it out on the surface of the water to attract attention from above. Whereas a person bobbing in the water is nearly invisible, the See/Rescue Streamer greatly increases your visibility so that you can be spotted from 1.3 miles away by an air rescue plane flying at an altitude of 1,500 feet high. It comes rolled up in a mesh bag or nylon webbing case. It's manufactured by Rescue Technologies Corp. in Hawaii.

4. **Inflatable SOS Flag**—an orange vinyl flag with the international distress black ball and square symbol printed on it; the perimeter is inflated for stiffness and floatation. You can hold this up vertically to attract attention from boats or lay it on the surface of the water for airplanes to see. It comes with

four pieces of rope. I suggest that when you use it, you tie one end to yourself to increase your visible mass and tie the other end to a See/Rescue Streamer.

5. **Signal Mirror**—a small, 2×3 inch or credit-card-size floating mirror with lanyard attached is best because it can fit in a pocket of your BC (buoyancy compensator), clothing or bathing suit. Of course, the larger it is, the greater the flash, and glass gives the most perfect reflection, but save that kind for the boat—you want polycarbonate because it won't break into sharp, dangerous pieces like glass will if it's dropped onto something hard. You don't want stainless steel either because it can get bent and the distortion will make it nearly useless. Also, even stainless steel can rust in saltwater. The surfaces of both stainless steel and polycarbonate (being as it's a plastic) will be marred if they're scratched, so keep your mirror covered and protected; a Ziploc bag is better than nothing. Overall, polycarbonate is the best compromise because it is stiff, corrosion-proof (provided the manufacturer, or you, properly sealed all edges, including a

hole), and lightweight. Signal mirrors come with or without a focusing hole to make it easier to aim. Some have a red reflective side, which makes its flash definitely intentional, distinguishing it from common accidental flashes produced by sun striking a windshield or bright work on a rocking boat. Some signal mirrors have directions printed on the back. *Before you need it, practice at home using it* so that it becomes second nature to use it correctly in an emergency. The very best are Rescue Reflectors, Inc. signal mirrors, which are handmade and tested individually. In an emergency, if you have nothing else, you might be able to use the reflections from some other shiny object, such as a CD, holographic credit card, wristwatch, or face mask—*but don't count on it!* www.equipped.org is the website for Equipped to Survive, Inc. It has an excellent discourse on signaling mirrors and other distress/rescue/survival equipment. I highly recommend you visit it.

Night/Darkness Signaling Equipment

6. **Flashlight**—small, regular, or large—it must be waterproof enough to withstand scuba diving depths. Modern flashlights are better than ever—brighter and longer lasting. You can choose ones with LEDs, xenon, halogen bulbs, lithium batteries, and even types requiring no batteries, like the magnet-shaking kind (especially good for the boat). It should have a lanyard so you won't lose it if you drop it. Select one with a simple on/off switch that won't go on by itself or make it prone to flooding; in addition, a hold-down switch for signaling SOS is nice but not necessary.

7. **Strobe**—strobes come in white, amber, red, and perhaps other colors of light, depending on the color of their lens. The pulsating light from a strobe is very good for attracting attention at night. Strobe sizes vary from tiny key-chain size to two or three inches wide by six inches long. There is even a combination model that has a strobe on one end and a flashlight on the other end. Whichever you choose, you

need to attach it to the upper part of your body (highest point, such as head, shoulder, or upper arm) so that it can be seen from a distance. Ideally, the strobe should have enough battery power to last three nights in a row. (Of course, you turn it off during daylight.) Again, you want something capable of withstanding normal or greater diving depths.

8. **Laser**—red or green laser light beams can penetrate the sky for long distances, so they make ideal signaling instruments. Now you can buy lasers that are truly waterproof. I own a red laser, manufactured by Saekodive. I've taken it scuba diving as deep as seventy or ninety feet, and it still works fine. Good ones, not the toys, are expensive, and the green costs twice as much as the red, but it's twice as good too. Imagine being a lost diver bobbing in the ocean at night, and you signal an airliner with your laser! Hopefully, the angry pilot will report you to the authorities.

Anytime Signaling

9. **Loud Whistle**—120-decibel minimum loudness. Storm and Fox Whistles are very loud. Whistles without "peas" (little wooden balls) inside are preferred because the peas might stick. Despite the claims, I've yet to hear a whistle underwater! Being shrill, whistles are in the high-frequency hearing range. (**Note:** there are now available underwater "quackers" for signaling your dive buddy. They hook up to your scuba tank and sound a bit like the insurance commercial's Aflac duck! However, if they work at all, they don't last long. Don't waste your money.)

10. **Small Mechanical Air Horn**—consists of three overlapping plastic tubes with a thin plastic membrane stretched over one end (the fragile membrane is protected by a grid). When you blow into the small hole in the side of the horn, a loud foghorn-like sound is produced. If your rescuers don't hear your whistle, they will probably hear this if they're close enough, as the low frequency sound carries well over water. This

WILD WOMEN ON THE WATER

horn is every bit as good and loud as a gas propelled air horn, with the advantage of never rusting and never running out of Freon. The smallest size presently being offered is $5\frac{1}{4} \times 1^{15}/_{16}$ inches. (Perhaps some-day someone will manufacture a three-inch size especially for divers.)

Other Essential Equipment

11. **Compass**—a submersible compass is vital for getting your bearings if you've lost sight of land. It can indicate which way to swim or help you avoid areas you know you want to stay away from. Try before you buy. The tiny watch band compass I tried out in the store wasn't very reliable; perhaps it was attracted to the steel shelving or the steel case of my watch. Standard-size compasses are quite compact anyway. To minimize, you might want a combination gadget, like a whistle with a compass on it.

12. **Tether**—a length of cord, rope, bungee cord, or strap, three to ten feet long, with quick-release clips on each end to keep divers together. You don't want to be separated

from your buddy by waves, current, fog, or whatever. With a tether, you can take turns sleeping without worrying about drifting apart. It is good to have a buddy to watch each other's back for strength, comfort, and moral support, but you can survive alone, as others have, if you keep your wits about you. A bungee cord is a particularly good choice because it can be used for a tourniquet or perhaps to propel a pole spear.

13. **Resealable Bag**—quart to gallon size, watertight, with a wide mouth to catch rainwater. It should be durable. You should have a means to keep it on your person, such as a lanyard or straps, or put it in a larger net bag. If it rains, be thankful you can take advantage of it instead of just being cold, wet, and miserable! Shipwrecked sailors have lived on as little as one cup of water a day.

14. **Knife**—any corrosion-resistant knife with a point will do. If you don't normally carry a dive knife, then place a small, probably folding, knife in your survival kit. (I have a titanium jackknife in my kit.) You can use it to cut materials and clean fish.

15. **Mesh Bag**—to keep it all together. Such a bag is self-draining and causes very little drag in the water. Stuff your bag of diver survivor goodies into your BC pocket or attach it to your backpack straps or onto a nylon canvas web belt you've designated for that purpose. **NOTE:** *Do not attach your survival gear to your weight belt!* In an emergency, if you have to ditch your weight belt, you don't want all your survival gear to go with it! Also, your special survival belt's buckle should be different from your weight belt's buckle so you won't release it accidentally; I like the square plastic squeeze sides-push-and-click buckles. After a day of diving, thoroughly wash, rinse, and let dry the bag and every component of it. Otherwise, salt crystals will form—they are sharp, and they can cut, corrode, and gunk up your precious life-saving equipment, rendering them useless. Be sure to lubricate metal parts and tools, like bronze swivel snaps and the knife, with WD-40 penetrating oil. Periodically check the integrity of the mesh and the connecting fastener; you don't want to lose your emergency equipment!

Nonessential Equipment

- **Neoprene Hood or Bathing Cap**—to keep your head warm, as much of the body's heat is lost from the top of the head. If it has a brim in the front, so much the better as it would be helpful in cutting down the glare on your eyes.
- **Waterproof Sun Block**—to reduce painful sunburn, especially on your face. Use SPF 12 or higher, but the higher the better. You want sun*block* instead of sun*screen*. Look for one that is UVA and UVB protective and has the longest water resistance time. Protect your lips also. A compact tube made for the lips can also be used on the skin of your face, although it might be sticky. Zinc ointment is a natural sunblock. You can buy a waterproof lotion that protects against stinging creatures in the ocean as well as the sun's rays.
- **UBF/UVR Swimmer's Goggles**—will protect your eyes from the sun's rays and also allow you to watch out for sharks underwater. This type of goggles can be found in dive shops.

An excellent website that lists and evaluates survival equipment is **www.equipped.com**. It is primarily for private pilots, but much of it equally applies to divers, sailors, and other outdoorsmen and women.

SURVIVING DANGER

What's the difference between a victim and a survivor? Well, a lot of factors, including luck, the situation, and determination versus just giving up. While initially they might panic, survivors quickly bring their emotions under control and start thinking rationally about how to save themselves. Here is a helpful mnemonic: PADI.

- **P**ray. Even if it's only a quick, informal "Oh God, help me!" do say it because you are going to need all the help you can get!
- **A**ssess the situation. What's happening? Are you being swept away in a current, going where? Orient yourself. If you are in the open ocean, away from inlets and such, and you are in the Keys (on the ocean side, not the Gulf of Mexico side), or Southeast Florida, or the Southeastern United States, then you in the Atlantic Ocean and that current is the gulfstream, and it is carrying you north. Land is west of you. Is the boat

sinking? Who or what is nearby that can help? Another boat? A lobster buoy? Can you stuff a pillow or your shirt into the hole to stop the leak? No? Then where's the life raft, can of water, and survival stash? Grab snorkeling gear, life vests, and ice chests—anything that can help you float or swim or survive. (Two fat men clung to an empty, overturned ice chest and successfully swam ashore eleven miles away!) Link a bunch of coolers together in a circle; not only will they give you and your crew better floatation, but the formation will present greater bulk, making it easier for searchers to see you.

- **Do** something! Scream, wave, swim over to that other boat or to those buoys and hang on tight. If there is nothing in sight, you might as well swim toward shore, which would be to the left of the direction in which you are being carried. You might get lucky; terra firma could be as little as one to three miles away. However, never abandon a floating boat unless you are sure you can make it and the boat is going to sink completely. If you miss this narrow window of opportunity, you will be carried so far out to sea that you may never be found. Weigh your odds quickly but well. Remember, when viewed from the sky, a boat without a wake is just a speck, and for all practical purposes, a human head bobbing on the water is invisible. On the other hand, one shipwreck survivor lived three months on a wooden raft before being rescued, and he wrote a book about it. See what's in your survival kit that can help you. Do something, but think of consequences before you act. One survivor diver said she purposely did *not* ditch her weight belt because she was wearing so many layers of neoprene rubber that she would have been *too* buoyant to swim properly; she would have bobbed helplessly in the water without making much headway.

- **I**nspire yourself. Let the thought of your loved ones inspire you to *live* for *them*. (Like Cristine Pistol, who had a baby boy to raise.) They'd be devastated if they lost you, and they need you. Inspiration can come in many forms. Even the opposite of love— anger or revenge—can inspire some people. One of my survival books told about a man who lived because he was embroiled in a divorce and didn't want his wife to get his assets! Be inspired by survivors who overcame incredible odds to live, like Valerie De La Valdene, who battled tremendous currents in shark-infested waters to reach a desolate Galapagos Island; Ignacio Siberio, an old man who spent a bitterly cold, stormy night alone in the ocean; and Cristine Pistol, who was nearly lost at sea at night. (I'll tell you their stories later.) They lived, and so can you.

THE PSYCHOLOGY OF SURVIVAL

Most survivors have the following in common:

- **A spiritual connection.** They believe in God and put their faith in Him. Or they believe in the universality of life, and that, living or dead, they are part of the cosmos.
- **A sense of humor.** They see the irony of their situation and can laugh about it.
- **An appreciation of the environment.** Even in their most dire straits, they recognize the *beauty* of nature around them, and it fills them with a sense of awe and wonder. They are also keenly *aware* of the present *condition* of the environment, any *changes* in the environment, and they look ahead to try to *predict* any future changes of the environment. Unexpected rain, mudslide, a drastic change in temperature, snow, blizzard, avalanche, thunderstorm, lightning, wildfire, or freak of nature can turn a pleasant day trip into a disaster or a nightmarish strug-

gle for survival. Be *flexible*; you may have to change your plans.

Judy O'Hara-Vetrick and Eileen Lomas-Fox, chairwomen in charge of the annual fall WWOW canoe and camping trip, didn't automatically assume we'd do the Peace River again as usual. No, they carefully did their homework first. After all, Florida had been hit by four hurricanes, some of them monstrous! They made phone calls, got on the Internet, and checked out websites. They learned the Peace River was out because it was too dangerous. It was at flood stage, and trees, dead animals, and large logs were swirling down it. Most of the rivers across the state were that way. But they located one that was said to be unaffected. They personally drove up to the Manatee River to check out the river, the canoe livery, and campgrounds. Fortunately, they found the Manatee River to be slow and peaceful and still lovely, and everything else was satisfactory. So they made the arrangements. They wisely avoided hazardous conditions through proper planning.

Valerie De La Valdene, a professional underwater cinematographer, had gotten so caught up in the experience of her environment that she failed to notice the danger of her environment. When suddenly she found herself surrounded by sharks, she surfaced to find herself completely alone! She was separated from the other divers and the boat by miles of strong ocean current that was rapidly carrying her out to sea. She thought she was going to die and screamed in panic, although there was no one to hear her. She had no idea where she was until an unusually large wave (God's help?) came along and raised her high enough to see land. At that point she realized she had to swim for it before it was too late or die. Valerie De La Valdene didn't want to die.

- **Inspiration.** The thought of their *loved ones* waiting for them at home spurs them on. When Cristine Pistol, years before she became a WWOW member, found herself adrift during a stormy, ill-fated, check-out night dive, only her prayers that she would reunite with her baby son Christopher kept her alive and struggling, as one after another, each "failsafe" device failed her.

Recalling *hero figures* may give strugglers hope that they, too, can do it. Even fictional characters can be real hero figures. *The Little Engine That*

Could—"I think I can, I think I can, I think I can!"—
is the classic children's book that made an indelible
impression on Valerie De La Valdene as a little girl.
It stuck with Valerie the adult, the heroic little train's
mantra becoming her own, inspiring her to overcome impossible odds. She was in the ocean for six
hours. This young woman swam alone through a
circling school of sharks for two miles against strong
currents toward a desolate Galapagos island.

- **Pattern repetition.** Dogged determination
  expressed by rote actions gives the brain a
  rest while keeping the mind under control.
  It does two things: prevents panic and makes
  physical progress at the same time. One foot
  at a time, scissors kick left, right, with the
  hands, reach and pull. Distract the mind of
  dreary business by reciting poetry in your
  head, singing to yourself, telling yourself
  jokes, or counting numbers. Anything to do
  the mechanics of survival without thinking
  about it. You don't want feelings of boredom,
  monotony, fear, and hopelessness to wash
  over you; it may discourage you and cause
  you to give up in defeat. You need to be a
  survivor, not a victim! Eventually, "I think I

can, I think I can, I think I can" becomes "I know I can! I know I can! I know I can!"

At last, Valerie De La Valdene reached the island. But it consisted of steep rock cliffs. The lowest point she could see was a rocky shore formation called the Washing Machine. No one before her had ever swum it and still lived to tell about it.

When adventures turn dangerous, the adventurer often has to accept pain and discomfort as the price to pay for survival. Valerie entered the Washing Machine.

Waves swept her forward and back and pulled her under. She was tossed and turned and churned. Rough rocky surfaces shredded her gloves and scraped her hands raw and bloody as she tried to control her body. Sharp rocks cut her skin. The agitation inside the Washing Machine bashed her rib cage against a boulder and busted a rib.

Finally, a giant wave hurled her up onto a craggy cliff. (God's help again?) She was bruised and bleeding, and had a broken bone, but she was *alive*!

When her rescuers came looking for her, she waved her extra-long orange free-diving fin to signal them. Obviously, it was an answer to someone's prayers.

So divers, survivors themselves, become sources of inspiration.

Cristine's Story

In 1987, Cristine Pistol and her husband Bobby took their Advance Open Water Certification. They went on a 45' diving boat for the last portion of their certification. The day was beautiful until the late afternoon, when it started changing.

As they left the dock, the seas were between 5 to 6 feet, increasing as time went. By the time they reached their destination, it was dark, and the seas had grown to 8 or 9 feet.

The dive boat crew told them to follow the line (rope) tied from the stern (back) of the boat to the bottom. Cristine's husband went next after the dive instructor, and then she followed. As they descended, the waves were getting bigger and bigger... and with time their flashlights stopped working, because water got inside. Cristine lost sight of her husband, but she had the rope in her hands, so she kept going and going.

She was never so terrified as after she kept going, she reached the end of the rope and there was nobody in front of her, and complete darkness!

But she heeded her training and dropped to the bottom to look for the anchor. She found it and proceeded to swim upward, following the line. As her head reached the surface, the bow of the boat was coming down from a wave, so she had to swim fast down the line to not get hit in the head.

All this time, her thoughts were that she did not want to leave her baby so soon (he was only 2 years old at the time), so she did not give up. She swam on the bottom some distance, where the waves were less, and came back up to look for the boat. To her surprise, the boat was nowhere around. It was dark, cold, and she was tired. Again, her training took over and she kept repeating to herself, "I can't give up!" So, she inflated her BC and lit the luminous stick attached to her BC and decided to wait and wait. She really thought her son would be motherless and her husband a widower, such was her despair... but she had to stay calm.

About half an hour later, she saw a small light at the distance, but being so short, no matter how much she waved they could not see her between the waves. Every time she tried to scream, more water went down her throat, so she tried to conserve her voice and kept her eyes glued to the small light approaching.

Another half an hour later, the light grew bigger and bigger and she realized they had the search lights on and they were calling her name. Boy, she was so happy to see that light finally zero in on her! It took some time for them to reach her, but there was her husband ready to pull her up and out of the water with tears in his eyes... She had never been so grateful to see the look of love and happiness in his eyes as she did that night!

I guess you can understand, that after all this time, she still won't dive at night nor does she have any desire to do so.

Another, local hero, is Ignacio Siberio, an eighty-year-old man from Tavernier, Florida. On December 11, 2004, he was out on the reef spearing fish while free-diving. The day was cold and windy. He shouldn't have been out, because there were small craft warnings. While he was busy spearfishing, the anchor ripped loose and his boat floated away. By the time he noticed it gone, it was already too far away for him to catch, even though he tried for hours. He spent the night battling eight-foot waves, twenty-mph winds, and a temperature drop to fifty degrees while clinging to lobster buoys. He wore only a shorty wetsuit, but fortunately it had a hood. He kept moving his legs to keep warm.

During the night, something bumped him (perhaps a shark?), but he kicked it away. After eighteen hours in the water, he was rescued the next morning by his great nephew, who refused to give up, even though the Coast Guard did.

Cristine Pistol, Valerie De La Valdene, and Ignacio Siberio are all heroes to inspire diver survival. If they could do it, so can you!

Possible Life-saving Tips—How to get away from a shark: If you have fish or bait on your person that has attracted a shark, drop it and swim away to safety, such as to a shore nearby or back to your boat. Keep one eye on the shark. If your diving buddy is nearby and unaware of the shark, try to notify him by banging on your scuba tank with your diving knife or speargun or honking with your quacker, preferably with prearranged signals. If you go to the surface, holler "Shark!" to your friends so that if anyone's in the boat, they can pick you up. Do *not* splash! Splashing will only attract the shark like a struggling fish would. Try to keep something large between you and the shark, like a bang stick (a power head on a pole of some kind, usually an aluminum pipe; the power head discharges a shotgun shell or large caliber bullet upon impact), large camera housing, or spear gun; if you have nothing else, you can take off your scuba tank and use it as a battering ram. The shark may be only curious or just passing through. But watch out for excessive, erratic behavior. Hostile, aggressive body language will be if he arches his back, lowers his pectoral fins, swims erratically, and opens his mouth. If he comes at you, dodge to the side and jab him in the eye or gill slits. A shark has a series of dots in a line on the tip of his nose; these are electrical sensors very sensitive to vibrations, and through these the shark can detect prey from a distance. Hit him as hard as you can on that area of his nose. If you have nothing in your hands with which to defend yourself, try pinching his nose; you might be able to stay away from his teeth by strong-arming him and hanging onto his nose with both hands, if that's the only chance you have. In a television documentary, a "shark wrangler" mesmerized sharks, *even great white sharks*, by stroking their noses! However, these particular sharks were swimming slowly and not acting aggressively.

Do *not* shoot the shark with your spear gun unless he's coming for you with his mouth open with the intention of biting you! In that case, fire a spear down his gullet! BeBe Hall of Plantation

Key did this and saved the lives of herself and her brother, Olympic swimming star Gary Hall, once when they were spearfishing. But bear in mind that if your spear shaft is attached by a line to your gun, you will lose your only weapon of defense. Also, any blood in the water will attract more sharks. However, if it's you or your buddy or the shark, and you have a bang stick, then by all means use it on a vital spot like the shark's heart or brain.

As final comments, if you frequently go spearfishing or surfing or diving in murky water, you might want to consider purchasing a *Shark Shield* from Australia, an electronic device worn on the leg, with a trailing antenna, designed to repel sharks by overloading the input from their nose sensors. Another product for repelling sharks is called Sharkbanz. It's a strong permanent magnet encased in plastic that you strap on your ankle or wrist.

Also, the Moses sole in the Red Sea exudes a natural secretion that repels sharks. Dr. Samuel "Sonny" Gruber, an ichthyologist who specializes in the study of sharks, discovered that sodium lauryl sulfate is chemically very similar to the *shark-repelling substance* from the Moses sole. The good news is that this *sodium lauryl sulfate* is a chemical commonly found in *liquid dishwashing detergents and shampoos!* So if you should see a school of sharks circling your buddy, you should play the brave hero, jump in the water, and squirt them away with a bottle of liquid detergent. Or maybe not. Well, you should *at least* throw the bottle to your buddy so he can defend himself!

Disclaimer: Sharks are unpredictable animals, so it's impossible for anyone to know for certain how they will act or react, therefore, we make no guarantees that these tips will always work for you.

Catch-All Concoction
(A vegetarian meal)
By Gail Feddern

2 C. green, red and yellow bell peppers, chopped
2 medium onions, chopped
3 cloves garlic, minced
2 carrots, chopped (optional)
1 can dry beans with liquid (your choice)
1 can kernel corn, drained
1 can tomatoes, drained
2 small cans tomato paste
1 small can water or broth
1 Tbs. olive oil
1 Tbs. butter or buttery substitute
seasoned salt (your choice)
vegetables, miscellaneous, chopped
rice, cooked

This is an ideal lunch to make prior to cleaning your refrigerator because it's the first step! Not only will it give you the energy to tackle the onerous task at hand, but it uses up the wilted but unspoiled vegetables found there. (Throw out anything furry, moldy, spotted, soft, or smelly! We're *not* serving petri dishes here.) Take the still-good vegetables and clean them up, peel them, chop them up, and add to the mixture. If it doesn't have to be vegetarian, you can chop and add cooked leftover meats to the cooked mixture.

Put fats in a large pan and cook peppers, onions, garlic, and carrots (if used) until done. Stir in the rest of the ingredients and cook a few more minutes. Serve with rice.

Mini Pizzas

By Gail Feddern

English muffins, split
1 tsp. olive oil, divided between two muffin halves
Italian herbs
garlic powder
tomato paste
cheese, 1 serving divided between two muffin halves

Preheat broiler. Assemble ingredients in the above order. Broil until cheese melts. Two muffin halves constitute a serving for one person, but you can make a lot of servings at once. This recipe will satisfy a crowd of pizza lovers. Children especially like it!

Note: To cut down on orphan items in your refrigerator, take a permanent marker and mark the container with the date you opened it. That way, you will know if you should throw it out because it's too old. For example, you won't need the entire small can of tomato paste if you are making just one serving of mini pizza. Mark the can, cover it, and refrigerate it.

Sunrise Surprise
(A vegetarian meal)
By Gail Feddern

1/8 to 1/4 C. pecan or walnut pieces
2 patties Morningstar Garden Burgers + 1/8 tsp. sage + 1/8 tsp. thyme + spritz of liquid smoke, or 4 vegetarian sausage patties or links
1 to 2 lb. chunk of calabaza squash
1 Tbs. honey (Keys mangrove honey preferred)
1 tsp. butter or heart-healthy margarine
Pam buttery cooking spray
0–5 calorie butter flavored pump sprayer, like I Can't Believe It's Not Butter spray
1 C. cooked thin spaghetti or vermicelli
salt and pepper to taste

Peel squash and cut it up into bite-size chunks. Spray a medium/large pan with Pam buttery spray. Place squash pieces in the pan, add butter or margarine, and cook until nearly done, stirring frequently. To keep it from burning, you can spray some more Pam, or add a little water, or cover. Break up veggie burgers or sausages and brown in pan with squash. If using burgers instead of sausages, add herbs and smoke flavor. Stir in nuts and honey. Stir in pasta. Season with salt and pepper and spritzes of butter spray. Heat and mix thoroughly. Serves 1 or 2 for breakfast or lunch. This is a healthy, low-calorie meal!

Helpful Household Hint from Carole Matuseski: *Save that sweet pickle jar of liquid!* Put peeled *hard-boiled eggs* in it. In a few days, you'll have delicious pickled eggs, albeit slightly green—all the better with which to celebrate St. Patrick's Day! Of course, your Dr. Seuss–loving grandchildren may say they don't like green eggs, with or without ham. (For Easter you can color some eggs pink with beet juice. —Ed.)

BEES IN YOUR BONNET

There are good bees and there are bad bees. Unfortunately, the bad "killer" or Africanized bees look to the naked eye just like the good bees. You should not exterminate bees without good reason, because bees are very important to the ecology and our economy and are needed to make much of the food we eat. For example, a bee has to pollinate an orange blossom, or an orange won't form. What's Florida without its oranges? And of course, honey is a delicious, naturally healthy treat. (Down here in the Keys we are especially blessed to have mangrove honey.) So please give the bees a break; besides all the regular bee diseases, they have a tough time surviving the mosquito spray plane, mosquito spray trucks, tracheal mites, Varroa mites, hive beetles, and now a new mysterious something-or-other that is causing them to abandon their hives!

So how *do* you tell the difference between good bees and bad bees? Well, the bad bees are very aggressive. They will attack you if you get within twenty feet of their hive, and the meaner they are, the more guard bees will attack and chase you for quite a distance. Those bees need to be exterminated professionally. Gentle bees, on the other hand, like the ones in my beehives, will let you stand quietly just a few feet from their hive, while they go diligently about their business. Unless they've set up a hive in your house or some other unwanted place, let them be. Also, you might not want them around if a member of your family is allergic to bee stings. If you must remove them, try to get a beekeeper to take them because maybe he can use them, and usually he will try to salvage the honey/honeycomb. If the bees are Africanized, he might just tell you to call an exterminator. (And no, I don't do bee removal. But I will sell you raw organic Keys mangrove honey if I have a surplus.)

What should you do if you are attacked by bees? *Immediately duck and run, and get inside a building or even a car.* Swatting at them with your hands only provokes them more, so try not to do it; wait until you get inside, then swat them dead with a rolled up magazine or newspaper. If you jump in the water, they may just wait for you to surface and then sting you. Unlike hornets, yellow jackets, and wasps, honeybees can sting only once per bee.

When she stings you, her stinger separates from her tail and sticks in your skin. A little pulsating sack of venom attached to the stinger spasmodically pumps the venom into the wound, so you don't want to unintentionally squeeze more poison into yourself by grabbing it to pull it out. Instead, scrape it away with your fingernail. If you have multiple stings, use something like the edge of a credit card to scrape them away. Then rub a cut, raw garlic clove on the spot to make the pain go away. (You can substitute garlic juice or a paste made of garlic powder and water, prepared garlic, or if there are a lot of stings, a cut raw onion.) An antihistamine like Benadryl will reduce the swelling. Of course, anyone who is dangerously allergic to insect stings should carry an antidote with them in a first aid kit.

Helpful Hints about honey: Pioneers utilized honey's natural antibacterial properties in dressing wounds, as well as in infusions for the sick to drink. Even some modern doctors successfully treat diabetic wounds with honey when antibiotics fail. *Honey never goes bad!* Do not refrigerate it, unless you want it to turn into sugar faster. To desugar honey, simply put it out in the sun or place the jar in warm water; the sugar crystals will melt back into liquid honey again. *Do not* give honey to babies under one year old because their digestive systems haven't developed sufficiently yet to handle it.

Quick Tuna Casserole
By Gail Feddern

This is the survival meal I taught my family to cook for themselves.

    1 box macaroni and cheese mix (I use Thrifty
        Maid from Winn Dixie.)
    1/2 stick of butter or margarine (1/4 C.)
    1/4 C. milk
    1 can of tuna fish, drained
    1 can of peas, drained

Make macaroni and cheese according to the directions on the box.

Add the tuna and mix well. Carefully stir in the peas. Makes 4 servings.

Tuna Casserole with Mushroom Gravy
By Gail Feddern

1 lb. box of macaroni

1 can Campbell's cream of mushroom soup (Do not add water.)

1/4 stick of butter or margarine (optional)

1 can of tuna fish, drained

1 cardboard pkg. of frozen peas

Cook the macaroni 8–10 minutes or until done. Drain well. While it's cooking, stab a package of frozen peas 3 or 4 times with a fork, or once with a knife, throw into a microwave and cook on high for 5 or 6 minutes. When done, combine pasta, butter, tuna, mushroom soup, and peas. Serves 4.

Note: In both recipes frozen peas and canned peas can be used interchangeably. Both recipes are really fast and delicious.

Possible Life-Saving Tip: Onboard your boat, at home, in your car, and in your hiking backpack, carry one of the *new medical dressings that stop arterial bleeding.* They come as gauze, powder, liquid, and bandage forms. They have saved countless lives on today's battlefields.

You never know when you might be called upon to use it; a limb could be caught in a rope or wire and severed (or nearly so), a shark can attack, or people can be seriously injured in a car accident. Some of these miraculous dressings use chitosan, developed from chitin, a natural polymer found in shrimp shells, other crustaceans, insects, worms, fungus and mushrooms. If I were living in a survival situation, I would be tempted to try to make my own to keep on hand in case of emergencies. It would not be sterile, and that could make it dangerous to use, but if I or someone else was going to bleed to death otherwise in a few minutes, I would take the chance, hope for the best, and try to deal with the consequences later. I would bake some shrimp shells or crab shells, grind them into a powder, bake them again in an attempt to sterilize the powder, and then pour it into a clean container with a stopper or tight lid or cap.

Henry Spaghetti

By Gail Feddern's Husband, Henry

This was Henry's survival food that sustained him throughout college. This simple recipe is *so* bad for your heart and arteries, but it tastes *so* good! It just may take two undertakers to wipe the smile off your face.

2 hamburger patties
1 stick margarine
1/2 lb. vermicelli or thin spaghetti pasta
Heinz catsup
salt

Cook patties and then break into pieces. Cook and drain pasta, but leave it in the pot. Add margarine to the hot pasta to make it melt. Dump in the cooked hamburger *and grease*, and stir it all up. Salt it to taste. Mix in half a bottle of catsup or enough to suit your taste. Serves 3.

The End

INDEX OF RECIPES

Legend: brown=meats
red=pasta
flesh color=poultry
blue=seafood

Breads

Desserts

Miscellaneous

Party Foods

Confetti Cheese Ball – Linda McGee, P. 41
Spinach Soufflé – Daryl Stone, P. 76
Crab Rangoon – Daryl Stone, P. 78
Cowboy Caviar – Cindy Strack, P. 99
Famous Smoked Fish Dip – Daryl Stone, P. 180
Simply Yummy Appetizer – Marie Henson, P. 184
Sun Dried Tomato Hummus Dip –
Brenda Bush, P. 192
St. Patrick's Day Pickled Eggs –
Carole Matuseski, P. 344

Salads

Taco Salad – Donna Hanson, P. 26
Twenty-Four Degree Salad – Judi Bray, P. 28
Roasted Potato Salad – Eileen Lomas-Fox, P. 36
Chinese Chicken Salad – P. 42
Cabbage Salad – Daryl Stone, P. 75
Spinach Salad – Daryl Stone, P. 77
Lobster Salad – Gail Feddern, P. 83
Beverly's Seven-Layer Salad – Beverly Hooper, P. 179
Malaysian Fruit Salad – Tanya
Feddern-Bekcan, P. 263

Side Dishes

Whipped Potatoes – P. 50
Mexican Corn Casserole – Gail Feddern, P. 195
Vegetable Compote – Gail Feddern, P. 197
Stewed tomatoes – Gail Feddern, P. 212
Anne Baxter's Aunt Delsie Mae's Candied Yam Casserole, P. 217

Soups

Six-Minute Pea Soup – Gail Feddern, P. 66
One-Minute Pea Soup – Gail Feddern, P. 68
Irma's Clam Soup – Irma Woodward, P. 151
Seafood Soup – Jane Martin, P. 159
Shrimp & Mushroom Soup – Cynthia McGregor (Boerner), P. 162
Lobster Bisque – Daryl Stone, P. 297
Cream of Mushroom Soup –
Phyllis Williams, P. 310

COOKING ABBREVIATIONS

C. – cup
doz. – dozen
lb. - pound
oz. – ounce
pinch or a dash – less than 1/8 of a tsp.
pt. – pint
qt. – quart
tsp. – teaspoon
Tbs. – tablespoon

ABOUT THE AUTHOR

Author Gail Feddern lives at her home on Dove Creek, Tavernier, Florida Keys. The bird on her head is wild, a Eurasian collared dove that loves people. One of her hobbies is beekeeping. She and her husband are marine life fishermen, catching saltwater tropical fish and invertebrates for the hobby aquarium trade. They have two cats.